ALSO BY ANNE GARRELS

Naked in Baghdad

PUTIN COUNTRY

PUTIN
COUNTRY

A JOURNEY INTO
THE REAL RUSSIA

ANNE GARRELS

FARRAR, STRAUS AND GIROUX

NEW YORK

Farrar, Straus and Giroux
18 West 18th Street, New York 10011

Grateful acknowledgment is made to Alexander Cigale for permission to
reprint his translation of lines from the poet Fyodor Tyutchev on page 123.

Library of Congress Cataloging-in-Publication Data
Garrels, Anne, 1951–
    Putin country : a journey into the real Russia / Anne Garrels.
        pages   cm
    ISBN 978-0-374-24772-0 (hardback) — ISBN 978-0-374-71043-9
(e-book)
    1. Cheliabinsk (Russia)—Description and travel.   2. Garrels, Anne,
1951—Travel—Russia (Federation)—Cheliabinsk.   3. Putin, Vladimir
Vladimirovich, 1952—Influence.   4. Cheliabinsk (Russia)—Social
conditions.   5. Cheliabinsk (Russia)—Social life and customs.
6. Cheliabinsk (Russia)—Biography.   7. Interviews—Russia
(Federation)—Cheliabinsk.   8. Political culture—Russia (Federation)—
Cheliabinsk.   9. Subculture—Russia (Federation)—Cheliabinsk.
I. Title.

DK651.C44G37 2015
947'.43—dc23

                                                                2015034644

Designed by Jonathan D. Lippincott

www.fsgbooks.com
www.twitter.com/fsgbooks • www.facebook.com/fsgbooks

1   3   5   7   9   10   8   6   4   2

To Vint, as ever with love

CONTENTS

PUTIN COUNTRY

ONE

CHAOS

On a midwinter morning in 2013, the Russian city of Chelyabinsk was blinded by a white streak in the sky. It lit up the late dawn and arced across the horizon, leaving a trail of smoke. Students at Lyceum 31 pressed their noses to their classroom windows to see "the unreal light." Minutes later, there was a huge blast. Solid windows merely shuddered, but across the city panes and TV screens shattered, sending shards flying. Car alarms were triggered, and the roof of a zinc factory partially collapsed. Around twelve hundred people were injured by the hail of debris. Amazingly, no one was killed.

Remarkable images immediately flooded the Internet, recorded by car video cams mounted on dashboards. These are commonly used to record the region's all too frequent traffic accidents and support insurance claims. What they recorded this time was the result of a sixty-foot-wide meteor approaching the earth. It came in undetected at roughly forty-two thousand miles an hour—twelve miles per second. It began to blow apart twenty-eight miles above the Chelyabinsk region, exploding with the energy of about five hundred kilotons of TNT, thirty times the power of the Hiroshima bomb. At its most intense, the fireball glowed thirty times brighter than the sun. Scientists say it was the largest rock to reach our planet since 1908, when another meteor crashed into Siberia's Tunguska River.

Fragments rained down all over the countryside, with the largest single piece punching a huge circular hole in the thick ice of Lake Chebarkul, a couple of hours' drive from the regional capital. There was no boom there, just a flash of light. Worshippers at the nearby Orthodox church continued with their service. Ice fishermen dozing off on the frozen lake were shocked out of their sodden reverie, but whatever had landed quickly disappeared in the watery depths, leaving only a gaping hole.

Eight months later, divers retrieved a half-ton piece of space rock. It broke into three pieces when it was lifted up. The largest piece now sits benignly under a Plexiglas dome in the regional museum. Compared with the colorful rocks indigenous to the Urals, glistening green malachite and deep purple charoite, the residue of the meteor is a dull lump, with sculpted pits where its molten material chipped off on its extraordinary journey.

The superstitious and the religious tried to find some meaning in this rare event. Wags suggested President Vladimir Putin's appointed governor, long the target of corruption allegations, had been fingered for his sins. What everyone agreed was that Chelyabinsk, a gritty industrial region a thousand miles east of Moscow, was again on the map, though for once the troubles were not man-made. Known to be one of the most polluted places on the planet because of a once-secret nuclear accident and choked by clouds of industrial waste, the area had suffered plenty of indignities. But residents looked on this natural event with a kind of pride and awe. Trade in alleged "space rock" flourished briefly. A local chocolate factory came out with a deluxe Meteor assortment.

Chelyabinsk had been on my radar since 1993, two years after the breakup of the Soviet Union, when a newly independent Russia was struggling for its survival. I had served many stints in the Soviet Union and the new Russia as a journalist and was then NPR's Moscow-based correspondent. As any Russian will tell you, Moscow is not Russia, and in the 1990s it was clear that the country's richest and most powerful city was racing even further ahead. Moscow is not just the capital and seat of government. It is also the financial, commercial, cultural, and entertainment center—Washington, New York, Chicago, and L.A. all wrapped into one. But most Russian citizens, including the members of many diverse ethnic groups, live elsewhere. Dispersed across a vast landscape, they both admire and resent the Moscow megalopolis. I decided I needed to find a place far beyond the capital's Ring Road where I could follow these citizens of the new Russia as they picked their way through the rubble of a political, ethnic, social, and economic earthquake.

Deciding to focus on one provincial area, I considered any number of towns and regions and finally let fate decide. Lacking a dart, I threw a sharpened pencil at the huge map of Russia in my office. It landed close to the center, making a small rip in a region that, like much of the country, had long been closed to foreigners but had recently opened up to the world. Given my silent pledge to go wherever the pencil point landed, my relationship with the city of Chelyabinsk and the surrounding region of the same name was sealed. I have been going there regularly ever since. It has indeed become my second home.

The size of Austria, and with a population of only three million, the Chelyabinsk region sits on the southern edge of the Ural Mountains. The word "mountains" is a bit of a misnomer. Worn by the ages, they are now really little more than humps, dividing the western, "European" part of Russia from Siberia. Far from Moscow and the Pacific alike, people here are proud to live in what they call the backbone of Russia, a place rich in minerals and coal, forests, fields, and lakes. They believe they have supported the country in war and in peace. But the cost has been exorbitant, and the region is still raw from the ravages of history.

That history continues. When thousands of middle-class Muscovites took to the streets in 2010 and 2012 to protest election fraud, corruption, and malfeasance, the rest of the country remained relatively silent. The Moscow-based international press corps made much of the capital's protests but ignored the heartland. In those days, should you have read the Western media, you would have been persuaded the country was on the edge of rebellion.

The foreigners' blindness reinforced my determination to continue charting events in the Chelyabinsk region. Like most of Russia, it's Putin country, and as I write, it has only become more so. The reasons are many and confused.

Most people unhappily remember what they call the "anarchy" of the 1990s, when lawlessness and declining living standards followed the collapse of the U.S.S.R. They are eager for stability and a sense of national pride, which they believe President Putin has delivered. They dream of a country worthy of their love and admiration. Many resent the West, which they accuse of hypocrisy and arrogance. It's hard to find anyone who sees an alternative to the status quo; a grudging complacency is more common. The opposition is fractured, anemic, and intimidated.

When I first arrived in 1993, Chelyabinsk was a depressing place, where people were alternately desperate, hopeful, and fearful as changes emanated from Moscow. The entire region had been closed to foreigners since the late 1930s because of its "secret" military and industrial installations. Now those state-owned, state-controlled behemoths, often employing tens of thousands, were among the Russian institutions most threatened by the emerging market economy. Suddenly the Chelyabinsk region was a part of the world. Sprung free from government subsidies, lacking the structure and orders they needed to be "competitive," the area's factories required major revamping and investment. Given domestic chaos and a lack of capital at home, this had to be Western investment, about which they knew nothing. "Profit" and "bankruptcy" were the new buzzwords. A whole new vocabulary and set of ideas were gripping the country, and Chelyabinsk, like much of Russia, was ill-prepared.

I was among the first foreigners to arrive in the city, and government officials were embarrassed by the lack of "acceptable" accommodations. There were none of the Intourist hotels, shabby and overpriced, that had catered to foreign visitors in the country's open cities. The only hotels were even more run-down, with irregular heat and water, so the local authorities insisted I stay in what had been a Communist Party guesthouse. It was only marginally better, with its standard narrow single bed, peeling wallpaper, and pink nylon curtains—and its distinct smell of Soviet antiseptic and cigarettes, a smell that still permeated the country.

New restaurants and casinos were opening in Moscow but not yet in Chelyabinsk. A few private clubs had begun serving the small group who had cash. There weren't any signs. You had to know where they were. The clientele, mainly men in black shirts and black ties, accompanied by babes who never said a word, looked as if they had just walked out of a bad gangster movie. These denizens were known as "mafia"—the word quickly adopted to describe the new criminal gangs that made their money running protection rackets across the city, shaking down shops, the few emerging private businesses, and the remaining factories. The head of the city's police department admitted his men were outgunned, outmaneuvered, or complicit.

The skies over Chelyabinsk were clear of the acrid smoke I had been warned of, but the newly clean air was both a relief and a threat. It meant that the steel, chemical, and armament plants on which most everyone depended were at a standstill. Workers weren't being paid or were paid in bizarre goods like crystal vases or industrial pipe their factories had received in barter deals. Many of the biggest plants, with thousands of workers, provided poorly made, costly materials for the Russian military, which had all but collapsed. Those in control plundered anything they could sell off, most often for their own benefit.

Miners, living in conditions that were appalling even by Soviet standards, were threatening strikes. Hospitals had run out of basic supplies and were relying on intermittent Western aid. Food was in short supply, and under every chair, bed, or couch people stored what they managed to cultivate, bottle, beg, barter, or steal. National GDP fell 34 percent between 1991 and 1995, a larger contraction than the United States saw during the Great Depression, and the decline hit hardest in cities like Chelyabinsk. The mayor feared galloping unemployment, unrest, and a budget crisis that would leave the city dark and cold. His worst nightmares did not come to pass, but it was a near miss. Though winter temperatures regularly hover below 0 Fahrenheit, the unseasonably warm winter of 1993 dramatically cut the city's heating bills, providing much-needed relief. Factories were ordered to keep most workers on the books, even if they weren't being regularly paid.

■

Like many Russian cities, Chelyabinsk was organized around its foundering factories, which in many ways were self-contained mini-cities: they had their own run-down apartment complexes, hospitals, clinics, and day-care centers. Now these facilities were unloaded onto the local government, which could not cope. The government in turn told residents they could privatize their dwellings. Those lucky enough to have a government apartment suddenly became owners, though just what that meant then was unclear to most except for the criminally inclined. Given the absence of credit and mortgages, there was no real estate market— except for those who were making a lot of cash. Gangsters preyed on the elderly, conning or killing them for their one-room apartments. Meanwhile, the state no longer provided apartments to those who had been waiting in line for them. The young, who often lived with several generations of their families in small apartments, were stuck.

For a minority, the late 1980s and the 1990s were a heady time of revelation and positive change. The new era offered the chance to make money and to right old and new wrongs. What were once nocturnal debates in cramped kitchens became open conversations. The first question you asked anyone was "What have you read?"—though teenagers quickly tired of the onslaught of memoirs about the Stalinist past and were much more absorbed by pirated DVDs piling up in the markets. On TV, the floodgates had opened, and Mexican soap operas and British detective series became a constant staple. When the *Vzglyad* (Outlook) program went on the air on Friday nights, the streets emptied as people tuned in to the latest political eruption. There was a searing satirical program called *Puppets*, which poked fun at everyone. In those first years, it was impossible to stop people from talking, but for many the new freedoms were as traumatic as they were delightful. Everything they knew and depended on was disappearing.

Even today, few Westerners fully appreciate how unpopular Boris Yeltsin and his circle of Westernized and Western-supported advisers had become by the time the doddering, drunk president finally resigned at the end of 1999. After a honeymoon with the West, when many Russians fell in love with America, they felt all the bitterness and anger of a jilted lover when it didn't work out as they had hoped. While the West and Yeltsin's team argued that the privatization campaign was necessary to put the country's assets into the hands of people who might get them working, most Russians saw nothing but closed, mysterious auctions, inside deals, scams, street crime, and the rise of a privileged mega-wealthy group of oligarchs, many of whom had come to economic power with hidden Communist Party funds. All the workers got were a few privatization vouchers, so-called shares. In their desperation to feed their families, most quickly sold off these shares for a song to those who unaccountably had access to cash.

As money concentrated in Moscow and its streets became clogged with foreign cars, the rutted roads of Chelyabinsk remained free from traffic, with rusted Zhigulis and Volgas the main means of transport. Informal outdoor markets took over from state stores. At these markets, locals, bundled up against the cold, traded what they could to make a few rubles—homemade clothing, cheap, untaxed imports from China and Turkey, and building materials of questionable provenance. Given rampant inflation, people took their profits to one of dozens of money exchanges that had sprung up selling dollars, which they then put under their mattresses. Everyone was tracking the daily dollar rate. All had become adept currency speculators to protect what little they had. It was exhausting and demoralizing.

For many in Chelyabinsk, and indeed in the rest of Russia, democracy and "reform" were becoming synonymous with hunger, crime, and a steep deterioration in social services. One of the most lucrative businesses was installing reinforced-metal apartment doors and triple locks to protect against growing theft and violence. Disillusion with the West's favorite, President Boris Yeltsin, propelled the people of Chelyabinsk to throw out his favored candidate for governor in 1996. An old-guard Communist was elected, but despite the vaunted claims that a new democracy was in place, with the attendant praise from Washington, Yeltsin rejected the results and put in his own governor. For a while, there was an utterly confusing situation with two competing governors in place. Eventually, the former Communist apparatchik prevailed.

In 1998, Russia defaulted on its foreign loans, and Chelyabinsk, still dependent on out-of-date, overstaffed factories, was hit hard again. "How much more can we take?" people asked as their jobs and savings evaporated yet again.

Former Soviet republics and the satellites of Eastern Europe appeared to be reveling in their new independence and new national identities, often casting themselves as Moscow's long-suffering victims. Only Russians seemed to be condemned for the Soviet past, even though many others had been complicit, or so it was felt. Russians watched as the European Union and NATO began to woo their former allies. The West, it appeared, was treating Russia like a loser that could be ignored or preyed upon.

When an increasingly incoherent Boris Yeltsin unexpectedly resigned, naming the relatively unknown Vladimir Putin as his successor, many Russians were relieved. A former KGB officer, healthy and articulate, Putin quickly exploited mounting popular anger. He knew what a decade of upheaval, humiliation, and nostalgia for the U.S.S.R.'s superpower status had done to the Russian psyche. In the south of the country, he brutally defeated Chechen rebels, who had earlier managed to fight Russia's military to a stalemate. Calling on his old friends in the security services, he used law enforcement to destroy his rivals. He blocked most opposition parties from registering and continued Yeltsin's game, once quietly condoned by the United States, of creating pliant, fake opposition parties. He abolished gubernatorial elections in favor of Kremlin appointments.

Most Russians didn't complain. They were suddenly benefiting from a boom in oil, gas, and raw material prices. Salaries were being paid. Social services improved. Pensions increased. Credit and mortgages were finally available, albeit at exorbitant rates for most. Rampant inflation was brought under control. Consumer spending soared. The price for all this—diminishing freedom and growing corruption—was one most seemed willing to pay. Exhausted by the revelations of glasnost, which for many amounted to washing the country's past sins in public, the public was sick and tired. It sat by passively as Putin took control of the nation's main TV stations and threatened the handful of independent media still struggling to do their jobs of informing the Russian public.

Throughout this period, I managed to visit Chelyabinsk pretty much on a yearly basis, though because of assignments to Iraq and elsewhere they were short trips. By 2012, I had retired from NPR and could spend months at a time there. It was perfect timing. President Putin's reign of stability seemed to be peaking, and a whole new set of issues was confronting the country.

TWO

STABILITY

It's 2012—a little over a decade since President Putin came to power. No one would mistake it for Moscow, heralded as the most expensive city in the world, but the center of Chelyabinsk is unrecognizable. I wander around on a glorious fall morning, the last before the snow. A cobbled pedestrian street has transformed the once colorless, run-down area. The former mayor who installed the cobbles also produced them, sold them to the city, and made a bundle. Between that conflict of interest and others, he now lives in luxury. But his record has been eclipsed by even more shameless conduct and even more improvements. The Russian economy has grown nearly tenfold under Putin, creating a consumer boom and an emerging middle class. Real incomes have increased. Poverty and unemployment nationwide have been cut in half.

The renovated city center has become a popular gathering place. On the cobblestoned street, the remaining prerevolutionary facades have been restored and now harbor elegant shops, restaurants, and bars. The street claims to be a copy of the Arbat, a famed walkway in Moscow. A dozen fanciful sculptures have appeared. Bronze musicians are frozen with their instruments next to real kids in designer jeans who suck on beer and busk for rubles that are finally holding their value. Giddy youngsters and their families pile into a stone carriage, posing for photographs taken with ubiquitous foreign-made smartphones. A statue of a beggar sits holding out a cap. Passersby toss in coins for luck. The change is then swiftly snapped up by some ragged drunks. Ever-superstitious Russians stand on a circle representing the zodiac, embedded in the pavement. They throw another ruble over a shoulder while making a wish. The same Russians who are devoted to astrological predictions and psychics now also wear crosses and drop by churches to ask a favorite saint for protection.

The Russian Orthodox Church, with its growing conservatism and power, is taking back long-confiscated properties, and everywhere churches are being restored or built. The contradictions between the mood of defensive nationalism and the appetite for all things Western are increasingly confusing. Friends start talking positively about a resurgent Russian identity, though they are hard-pressed to explain what they mean. The state-run media have begun to broadcast more and more anti-U.S. material, but all the shops and restaurants have foreign names, a stamp of quality and service.

Foreign words have been absorbed into the Russian language for centuries, but now the list has exploded. It includes just about every term used for computer technology ("browser," "upgrade," "provider," "hacker," and "chat," to name but a few) as well as "smailik" to refer to the round grinning emoticon on "e-mails." The stock market is similarly full of familiar-sounding words like "market call," "broker," and "bonus." English words seep into everyday speech with "cool" Russians now going "shopping." They buy an apartment through a "realtor," see a "receptionist" before reaching the "manager" to check out "price lists." Russians buy a car from a "dealer" for their "girlfriend." The proliferation of Russian-accented English words transcribed into Cyrillic letters is mind-boggling. The "restaurans" advertise "kreizy menus" to lure in people for "biznes lanches." The new rich live in "taoon haoozes" or "kottedges," a somewhat fanciful word for the new mini-mansions. This all drives some populists in Russia's parliament "kreizy," but "oh my God," another new addition, they have so far been unable to stanch the flow.

Along the Kirovka walkway, an enormous plastic ice cream soda lures customers into Pretty Betty, a replica of an American diner, complete with waitresses attired in 1950s-style bright yellow dresses, bobby socks, and sneakers, where "gamburgers" and "shakes" are in demand. A few doors down, the more sophisticated Wall Street Café is full of young professionals sipping cappuccinos and single malt. Elegant eateries in the neighborhood with names like Venice, Basilio, Deja-Vu, Avignon, and Titanic, decorated to look like the ill-fated liner, cater to the flush. More affordable Japanese and Chinese restaurants, their names in bold Western letters, are all the rage, with sushi the dish du jour.

The Rome, OK Karaoke, and Meet Point are just a few of the clubs packing in the fashionably attired night owls. At the McQueen restaurant and bar, the band opens with "Oh, Pretty Woman" sung in flawless English. When I later talked to the four musicians, indistinguishable from their Western counterparts in jeans and T-shirts, we had to quickly turn to Russian because lyrics were the extent of their English-language ability. Their repertoire is almost exclusively British or American rock songs, and they are among the most popular local groups, regularly hired by factories to celebrate annual fests such as Police Day, Metallurgical Day, and Tank Day. Their chance to really make some money comes when they play weddings and birthday parties for the newly affluent, who have generally made their stash in real estate and construction. Recently, they tell me, the "new rich" have become "more cultured." It is no longer fashionable to throw their money around in the vulgar, garish way they did in the rough-and-tumble days. The glitter and gangsterish black shirts of the early years have been replaced by Ralph Lauren.

Clothing stores, from Chanel, Max Mara, and Escada to more affordable chains like H&M, sell Western apparel for the stylish Russian women who effortlessly stroll the cobblestones in four-inch heels, which just make their already long legs seem endless. The new generation of Russian women has access to the best makeup, salons, spas, and fitness clubs (including Curves), not to mention plastic surgery. It's a far cry from the babushkas of yore.

Once the country was awash in the sickly sweet smell of Moscow Nights. Now shelves groan with a choice of perfumes and unguents. In one shop, a young man approaches the salesgirl for advice. She shows him a new scent. "Would you use that?" he politely asks, using the formal version of "you." "Tell me honestly." "No," she replies. He then asks what her favorite is. She thinks for a minute and then runs to a shelf, returning with a bottle. "I'll take it, then," he says. Minutes later, he returns with his purchase, wrapped in gift paper. He hands it to the salesgirl with the words "This is for you." The other shoppers smile and edge away, leaving them to continue the conversation on their own.

Back on Kirovka, travel agencies are everywhere, offering a booming business in cheap tours to Egypt, Turkey, Thailand, and Dubai, where enterprising resorts have learned to cater to the mass of Slavic travelers seeking sun and fun. For those tired of these destinations, South America looms. Posters aimed at the more adventurous suggest Machu Picchu. For the well-off, real estate agents advertise apartments in Spain and Miami.

Where not long ago there wasn't a single decent hotel, there are now many, some built by locals, others the franchises of American and European chains like Holiday Inn and Radisson. They cater to Russian and foreign investors, Western consultants looking for contracts to transform local industries, and traveling sports teams who come to challenge Chelyabinsk's hockey and judo stars. The most ostentatious hotel, aptly called the Grand, is overdecorated in marble, velvet, and tassels to reflect the glories of the 1920s, glories Chelyabinsk never enjoyed. All the hotels have one thing in common: their owners or partners are in the government or have close, very close ties to it. Access to what was not long ago state land is a murky business, and public auctions are easy to fiddle with, with the right contacts. This is Russian "entrepreneurship"; to maintain the necessary contacts, you pay the minions of the fiddler, who is ultimately Vladimir Putin.

As I wander through Chelyabinsk on this late fall day, I happen on a biker gang, hanging out in the square next to the main post office. They are preening in their leathers and petting their expensive Yamahas and Harleys. Oleg Aleikhin, in his mid-fifties, is by far the oldest and best turned out of the group. The relative of a senior official in the city government, he readily admits he makes his money as a fixer for shady land and property deals. He offers me a ride. It's too good an opportunity to miss because it's rare to chat with someone in the game. I agree and hop on the back. We speed off to a restaurant deep in the middle of Gagarin Park, where he's clearly well-known. He introduces me to his friend and business partner Andrei, as well as to two beautiful teenage girls named Polina and Vika. They are not thrilled to see me.

Oleg says he is helping the girls with their problems, though just what these might be remains somewhat of a mystery. While he downs shots of vodka, they flick their long hair, restlessly finger the Orthodox crosses around their necks, and listlessly play with their cell phones, alternately texting and checking the Russian version of Facebook. All I manage to extract from them is that their respective parents are divorced, and though only sixteen they are living with boyfriends in the city, where they attend prestigious high schools. Oleg and the girls then disappear. Andrei explains it could be a while before they return because they are having sex in the restaurant bathroom. He tells me they are not hookers but screwed-up teenagers. I jot down his number, hoping for further explanations, and leave for another appointment. Attempts to contact Andrei again are met with deflections, alleged illness, trips, and lies. I later bump into Oleg again, and he agrees to drop by my hotel.

This time, Oleg has traded his motorcycle for an expensive foreign car with all the bells and whistles. The corrupt property and land business, courtesy of his relative, is obviously doing well. He swaggers into the café, his fingers laden with huge rocks. He wears a massive fur hat and an ostentatiously expensive leather jacket with fur collar. The waiters can barely disguise their shock that I am meeting someone like this. While most well-off Russians have learned to be more discreet, Oleg's style remains "Russian mafia." Apart from continued hints about his business activities, he provides no useful information. He appears to have met me because he has been turned down for a U.S. visa and hopes I can help. When I explain that I cannot, he remains confident that his well-placed relative will save the day. So much for Oleg, but it takes a lot of toads to find a few princes.

As I navigate my way through the city, people are friendly, and when they learn I have been here many times before, they are quick to ask, "Haven't the roads improved?" They have, though the cost per mile has been astronomical given the corruption involved. People shrug off the price tag, saying at least there are now highways. I am regularly urged to compliment the new park, the new hockey rink, the malls, and the supermarkets offering a selection as good as, if not better than, my local Stop & Shop at home. With mortgages now available, albeit at a steep 20-plus percent, the real estate market has taken off. Those who were able to privatize their state apartments or crude village houses have sometimes watched their property soar in value, providing ballast in a long economic storm. By registering family members in their apartments, parents and grandparents can bequeath their property with no taxes and provide a safety net and nest egg for some in the younger generation.

On the northwest edge of the city, far from the downtown factories, the skyline is cluttered with cranes. An entire new district of apartment blocks is rising. It is a frantic effort to resolve the housing crisis, one of the Soviet Union's lingering legacies.

They are much better built than the crumbling barracks, dormitories, crude wooden houses, and Soviet complexes that are situated next door to the vast, filthy plants. There are also new clusters of attractive "taoon haoozes" in neighborhoods with English names like Green Park. Those first mini-mansions, styled as crenellated fortresses, complete with turrets, have become more refined and tasteful as Russians travel, gobble up *Architectural Digest*, and hire foreign designers or a new generation of foreign-influenced Russian decorators.

With access to credit—and everyone now lives on it—many apartment owners have done what they can to turn their flats into something more individual, more comfortable, and more "Western." After they install criminal-proof outer doors, the next step is to replace peeling, drafty windows with sleek thermal panes. A fortune has been made in glass. Tempting banners stretch across roadways advertising "Italian bath tiles and fixtures" and "European kitchens." IKEA, several hours away by car, has become a regular destination. Washing machines are now a regular feature, though dryers remain a luxury. After a trip to the United States, where she grew accustomed to tossing damp laundry in a dryer, one relatively well-off friend came home declaring she'd had enough of dripping sheets draped around the living room. Friends now constantly drop by to do their washing and—more to the point—drying.

Across the city, small to medium-sized businesses that supply the consumer boom and construction industry have proliferated. They are no longer subject to the criminal shakedowns of the 1990s, and unlike "the big guys," they can generally avoid political pressure as long as they don't rock the wrong boats. Even so, the corrupt, inefficient, and overly complicated bureaucracy remains a serious, time-consuming, and expensive impediment.

When I ask for an example of what a new enterprise can be in Chelyabinsk, I am sent to a factory. I slip and slide on the icy pathway past security guards toward a bouquet of balloons celebrating yet another year in business for the Chelyabinsk Compressor Plant. The yard is bustling, full of bright orange units ready to be shipped.

Albert Raisovich Yalaletdinov, general manager and owner of the plant, had been a professor of agricultural technology when the economic crisis of the early 1990s hit and his salary evaporated. Like everyone, he started trading in whatever he could to support his family. He also started looking for new opportunities. One day in 1996, he saw a notice in a newspaper. "A compressor has been stolen from a building site. If anyone has information on its whereabouts, there is a reward." For some reason, this piqued his curiosity. He didn't know anything about compressors and started to investigate. This was before Internet access, and Yalaletdinov spent hours in the local library, and then he traveled farther afield.

Compressors, he learned, use medium and highly compressed air to power pneumatic tools like jackhammers and drilling equipment. It turned out that Soviet-made compressors had been produced in what was now independent Uzbekistan and production there was in trouble. There was a need for better reasonably priced Russian-made equipment. Though there was no credit available, he and some friends set about designing and building their first compressor. It needed a lot of reworking. To support the project, they continued trading in scrap metal and tires, anything that would bring in money. They got hold of one of the many abandoned factories that had been stripped and was full of trash. Everyone pitched in to clean it and install heat and water.

In 1998, after what Yalaletdinov calls two years of trial and error, his team produced their first compressor. That was the year Russia defaulted on forty billion dollars in debt and devalued its currency, wiping out the life savings of millions of people, including those trying to create new businesses. Yalaletdinov hung in, and in 2002 he finally got access to bank credit.

He now has four hundred employees, who are well paid by

local standards and who have faith in their management. Sales are growing, and Yalaletdinov continues to plow profits back into the company. A taciturn man in his fifties, Yalaletdinov defies the usual description of "new Russian." Far from flashy, he refers to the success "of the collective" and hands me a book charting the hard-won achievements of his workers, the ups and downs, and the celebratory company picnics. He immediately warns me, "I don't talk much; I work." He is courteous, though not friendly. He is precise and somewhat stern. He doesn't talk politics, but he does express frustration with the country's continued reliance on oil and gas at the expense of new enterprises like his. He laments the demise of vocational schools, describing how hard it is to get young workers with even minimal skills. In the 1990s, when trade schools didn't pay faculty and factories seldom paid workers or paid them badly, talented people fled industry for professions like law, banking, trade, and construction.

I ask to what degree Yalaletdinov has to "show loyalty," a discreet phrase for the payoffs to the regional government many businesses must pay in order to survive. He says if you want to obtain something illegally, then you need to take part in politics to some degree, but if you work openly, you don't need it. "America had its period like this," he says. "We will work it out. Don't worry."

When I push him to describe the scale of corruption, he calls it enormous. When I push harder, he elaborates. He provides compressors for road building, railroads, and the oil industry, all enterprises largely controlled by the state. Government officials regularly demand fake, inflated receipts so they can skim off the difference. He says he won't play ball. Instead, he sells to a middleman. "What he does is his business. My business is to make good compressors at proper prices." After years of struggle, Yalaletdinov says that foreign companies are now increasingly interested in his compressors.

Those who want true economic development cite Yalaletdinov

as an example of the future, when optimists hope more and more honest Russian businessmen will reject threats and blackmail by the government. For now, most everyone seems apathetic, cowed, or bought.

In 2012, corruption even by official statistics was eating up one-third of the state budget. Putin had declared war on graft, and there was barely a town in the Chelyabinsk province where the city manager had not been arrested. Even some regional ministers were under investigation or behind bars. That should have been encouraging, but no one was encouraged. Those whom I spoke to believed Putin's "war" had been a calibrated fight.

Celeste Wallander, an astute Russia watcher, has described the system as a giant Mexican standoff where all the antagonists hold pistols aimed at one another. Those pistols, one could say, are loaded with *kompromat*, the Russian term for compromising material. Everyone has the goods on one another. If you are arrested and convicted, it's either because you were outside the system or because you stole more than is allowed and did not share up the chain. Almost no one who is arrested implicates others or "does a deal with the prosecution," because to implicate others would only make things worse. People keep their mouths shut, hoping to win a sweeter deal with their silence. They are also concerned that if they talk, their families will suffer.

■

Chelyabinsk's biggest problem is its legacy of huge Soviet plants that have failed to modernize. After years of struggling, many, despite the boom in oil and raw material prices, are finally dying. Provincial towns that are dependent on only one factory or exhausted mine now face extinction. Most worrisome, Mechel, the city's steel and mining giant, is in serious trouble. But even though Putin personally had much to do with its troubles, he is not blamed—just as he is not blamed for failing to diversify a Russian economy that relies too heavily on oil and gas revenues. Perhaps he escapes responsibility because of a compliant media or public confusion about international trade. Or perhaps it's because many cannot imagine who could possibly replace him.

Until 2008, Igor Zyuzin, the billionaire CEO of Mechel, did his best to shun the limelight and avoid politics. He clearly knew what happened to other "oligarchs" who opposed Putin. But Putin was reportedly irked that he was not more loyal. Complaints from other industrialists that Mechel was selling coking coal abroad for less than at home increased his ire. The price was set by legal long-term contracts, but that didn't matter. Putin demanded Zyuzin attend a government meeting. Zyuzin said he could not because of illness. In his inevitably snide way, Putin said, "Of course, illness is illness, but I think Zyuzin should get well as soon as possible. Otherwise we will have to send him a doctor and clean up all the problems." The medical help Putin had in mind was to come from the prosecutor's office and the antimonopoly service. The public rebuke of Zyuzin, followed by unsubstantiated charges that his company had fixed prices and harmed the Russian economy, had an immediate effect. Mechel's share price tanked, wiping some six billion dollars off the firm's value overnight. The entire Russian stock market then fell by 5 percent, the start of a downward spiral soon made far worse by the global financial crisis. For Putin, what mattered most was to demonstrate who was in charge.

Not long thereafter, Putin said he regretted that his attack on Zyuzin and Mechel had led to a fall in the firm's capitalization. As if talking about a recalcitrant child, he said Zyuzin is now "behaving." Lest the message was not clear, he warned other major companies to listen carefully to the state. By then, the damage to Mechel was done and the company's fortunes declined.

■

My 2012 visit to Chelyabinsk was suddenly interrupted after a couple of months, when I still had several weeks left on my visa. It was still pitch-black when the ring of the hotel phone woke me up at 6:30 a.m. A clearly distressed receptionist said someone wanted to see me. Shaking off what little sleep I had managed that night, I staggered into the lobby, thinking my driver had perhaps arrived much too early for a planned trip. Instead, the receptionist nodded nervously at two men I had never seen before.

I knew immediately who they were. I had seen the type many times before, cops in plain clothes that did nothing to disguise their true identity. The leather coats were standard-issue uniforms. The blank look was typical of their ilk.

They flashed their badges and said I was to go with them to the Federal Migration Office for some questions. When I tried to delay the visit for a day, it became clear this was not a request but a demand. "It will be quick," they said, and that's all they said. As I threw a coat over little more than pajamas, the receptionist, out of sight of our dawn visitors, asked in a terrified whisper if I was all right. She quickly scribbled the hotel number in case I needed it. She sensed what I didn't want to sense.

I was initially most concerned about having to cancel a long-awaited interview. After all, I had a legal visa. I was properly registered. I had been in Chelyabinsk for two months, working on this book. I had interviewed dozens of people, including several officials, explaining to all that I wanted to chart how Russia had developed over the past couple of decades through the prism of this industrial city.

The hours ticked by, and the questions turned out not to be "quick." My case officer wrote all my answers in painstaking longhand while others milled around, silently coming and going. I was fined for allegedly violating the terms of my visa. I was given no explanation but was initially relieved when I was told I could stay on in Chelyabinsk. But then I was left to sit, and my dossier grew fatter and fatter as papers mysteriously appeared from other rooms. Eventually, I was driven to another building in the center of town, which happened to be next door to the Federal

Security Service, or FSB, the heir to the KGB. I was ushered in to meet the head of migration. A tall, handsome man with expressionless icy blue eyes, Colonel Sergei Riazanov was in full uniform. (When I later looked him up on the Web, he was always shown in a suit.) He did not stand as I entered. He refused to shake my hand. He was surrounded by the group of men and women who had been silently collecting papers all day. The signs were bad. With no preamble, he told me I was to leave Chelyabinsk in three days and leave the country altogether in five. When I asked for an explanation, and a chance to challenge this order, his sneering reply dripped with sarcasm: "We are not yet as democratic as the U.S., and here you are not permitted a lawyer." When I protested that I was "law-abiding," he tapped my swollen file and referred to my first assignment to Moscow as a correspondent for ABC News thirty years earlier. That too had ended in expulsion. But that was 1982, in the Soviet Union, a different country, a different era. Then I had covered the dissident movement. I was accused of but never charged with espionage and subsequently expelled. Expulsion in those days was not uncommon for journalists who had spent more than two years in the U.S.S.R. and spoke the language. I had since been allowed back into the newly independent, newly "democratic" Russia many times and worked there regularly. I had been to this region a dozen times. What had happened this time? What nerve had I struck? Did someone decide that questions about what makes Russians tick were just too dangerous? Did someone make a phone call? And if so, who and why?

I thought of all the people I had come to know over the years: factory workers, shopkeepers, and successful businessmen; pimps and prostitutes; teachers, doctors, and social workers; Christians and Muslims; human rights activists and leaders of civic groups.

The first reaction from friends was "Weren't they just asking for a bribe?" When I laid out the scenario in more detail, they

acknowledged the usual Russian solution to a problem had probably not been within reach and that something more was at play.
But what? Did the authorities not want me witnessing a major
local corruption scandal that was unfolding? Were they concerned
about a nasty fight between the Kremlin-appointed governor
and the Kremlin-appointed chief judge, who were busily trading allegations of corruption? Perhaps I was a victim of the
growing anti-American campaign? Moscow is used to foreigners,
but perhaps provincial authorities were simply unaccustomed to
having an outsider digging around. As my friends speculated
further, I could see they were getting nervous, wondering what
was now in *their* dossiers. They were embarrassed to be nervous.
This wasn't the way it was supposed to be anymore. I felt what
I had not felt since Soviet times—concern for them, a fear that I
had inadvertently put them in danger. Some who had readily
given their full names in interviews just a few days before asked
that I no longer identify them.

THREE

IDENTITY

I had despaired that my expulsion from Chelyabinsk, along with the veiled allegations that I was a spy, would mark the end of my decades-long Russian travels, but to my amazement I continued to get visas. And to my continued surprise, my nemesis, Sergei Riazanov, the head of migration, was later arrested for taking bribes "on a major scale." As a result, I was able to keep in touch with the people I'd met in Chelyabinsk, including Irina Korsunova, a thirtysomething magazine editor. When I returned, we met in her office over sushi and pizza. She was clad in a sleek brown dress and fashionably cut long boots. She is an editor of an equally glossy magazine. Subsidized by the regional government, it promotes Chelyabinsk for potential investors, casting it in a fantastical light. Were you to flip through it, you would get the impression you were in Berlin, not a beleaguered, corrupt Russian industrial city. But there is a tiny part of the city that can afford the lifestyle promoted by the magazine, and Irina wants to see only the best here. She believes Russia has been and can again be an example for the world and that Western criticism merely reflects a desire to see Russia back on its knees. Despite all its current problems, she anticipates that Russia, with its natural resources, huge expanses, and talent, will once again be a country to be fully reckoned with.

To speak with her is to encounter a fierce defensiveness and many contradictions, but that is the point. Russians are trying to figure out who they are and where they fit into the world. Their embrace of much of Western culture and the selective denial of what doesn't fit into the official "Russian" model seldom make sense.

At one level, Irina could not be more Western. Her mother quickly took advantage of the opening to the West, became a successful businesswoman, and sent Irina to an elite Swiss finishing school. Irina traveled widely. She dresses in the finest European clothing. Married to a successful engineer, she is solidly middle-class and delighted that her son now has access to a range of Western consumer goods and technology that she never had as a Soviet child.

Even so, Irina harbors a resentment, almost an outright hatred of the West. She is a proud Russian who firmly believes Russia gave the best to the world while getting little in return. She also believes Japanese businesses and technologies are based on Soviet-Russian research. She says Chinese sport is now among the best in the world because it is based on Soviet sport techniques. She regrets the breakup of the Soviet Union and blames Western-imported corruption for destroying what was best about her country. She represents many I have met in Chelyabinsk. They are sick of beating up on themselves. They are sick of their country's being seen as nothing more than a mafia-ridden kleptocracy— even though they are the first to complain about corruption. They are sick of the West's beating up on them for their sins, especially now that they are more aware of Western sins.

In the absence of a national idea, Russians have fallen into blaming outsiders instead of dealing with the issues at hand. In the past, Russians have been at their best when facing an invading enemy: Sweden in the eighteenth century, Napoleon in the nine-teenth, or the Germans in 1941. Today the government, church, and state-run media rail against a more shadowy enemy, "foreign influence." These powerful forces have had considerable success in planting suspicions about a U.S.-Western conspiracy to under-mine a weakened Russia.

Russians' belief in their rightful place in the world is rooted in their turbulent history—a history of suffering, pride, and con-troversy that Chelyabinsk knows well. The city was founded in the eighteenth century as a garrison when the tsar's military moved into the uncharted east of the continent, heading toward Siberia and the Pacific. The tsar's forces expropriated land from the in-digenous Bashkirs and Tatars, nomadic Muslim herdsmen. The local historian Vladimir Bozhe, who has painstakingly documented these events, compares them to the bloody conquest of the American West. Most Russians I have met with, even the educated, have never heard of the expropriation or deny it hap-pened.

In the nineteenth century, Chelyabinsk became a trading center that connected the expanding Russian Empire and China. Remnants of the merchants' two-story wooden houses still dot the city center. Some of these elaborately carved ginger-bread confections have been restored, but most molder, their roofs caved in, waiting for the inevitable land grab. The Russian Orthodox Church soon followed the military outposts, and a sprawling convent complex with soaring onion domes came to dominate the growing town. Only photographs remain, as the vast convent was later blown up by Stalin's henchmen and re-placed by a stark parade ground, still graced with a large statue of Lenin.

It's been a story of boom and bust. In the late nineteenth cen-tury, the railroad drove through on its way to Siberia. The popu-lation quickly grew from seventy-five hundred to seventy-five thousand. Though technically forbidden to live outside certain designated areas of Russia, Jewish tradesmen moved here because of the expanding business opportunities. They were needed and largely tolerated. A synagogue was built in 1905. It would not be long, though, before the revolution swept through.

The 1917 revolution and subsequent civil war put a brake on development. The new Soviet authorities repeatedly confiscated the region's harvest, and widespread starvation set in. The historian Vladimir Bozhe estimates tens of thousands died in the Chelyabinsk region, decimating the local population. Repression of religion was more draconian than in many other places. Though Soviet law dictated that each confession have one place of worship in each community, Chelyabinsk was left with only one Orthodox church. Mosques, the synagogue, and churches for other Christian denominations were all shut down. The local Soviet leadership proudly declared it would be a "godless" city.

Moscow then decided the region would become an industrial center because of the local mines and mineral wealth, but there was no labor force left. In the early 1930s, workers and specialists had to be found to realize Moscow's plans for expanding and building metallurgical and chemical plants as well as a huge new tractor and tank factory, a centerpiece of Stalin's first five-year plan. Many brought here were political prisoners under guard. Others were kulaks—so-called rich peasants—who had been dispossessed of their tiny holdings, imprisoned, or exiled.

When war broke out with Germany in 1941, more prisoners were sent here to work, this time Soviet citizens of German descent who had lived in the country for generations but were suspected of being potential spies. Using records that were finally opened in the early 1990s, the historian Elena Turova has documented thirty-eight thousand Soviet Germans who were sent to Chelyabinsk: "They brought them in the midst of winter and dumped them in open ground where they began to dig underground hovels for shelter, while at the same time they were required to build the metallurgical plant." She remembers coming across the file card of a young boy who was shot because he didn't fulfill the daily "norm." The death rate was high from punishment, cold, hunger, and illness. "When they died, they just sent in more exiles who had first been sent to Siberia and Kazakhstan. Initially, it was men, then teenagers, then women who had to leave their children behind in the care of God knows who."

Moscow and the local government have provided no funding for Turova's careful, painstaking documentation. Money came from Germany, in the more open 1990s and early years of the twenty-first century. As Turova transferred the information from the yellowed, detailed Stalin-era archives to a computer database, she often felt physically sick. She was hit by conflicting emotions: horror at the brutality of her government, yet pride at her countrymen's ability to build an arms industry and push back Hitler. And as she pored through the newly opened archives, she discovered her own grandfather had been shot in 1931. According to the documents, someone overheard him singing some kind of ditty that was deemed anti-Soviet. He was taken away and never heard from again. Turova's mother never spoke about him lest the family be tainted by his alleged "treason."

Such once-hidden stories can be told by just about every family in the city. But the outrage that was frequently expressed in the 1990s has dimmed. Russians are now being told to ignore the mass killings and concentrate on Stalin's development of the country and its victory, against all odds, in World War II. The message is clearly that the end justifies the means. Volunteers who in the late 1980s and the 1990s collected information about victims of repression, hoping to get them compensation, now say, "We live in the shadows." Many were members of Memorial, a historical and civic rights organization dedicated to preventing a return to totalitarianism. It has come under attack by the Putin authorities because, as one leading member said, "the organization is on the wrong side of Putinism, specifically the idea that Stalin and the Soviet regime were successful in creating a great country." Memorial has closed its doors in Chelyabinsk.

But back to history. Chelyabinsk was at the center of the war effort. The wartime population exploded. Workers and armament factories that had been located close to the front were moved here, beyond the reach of Hitler's air force. For a while, it was proudly known as Tankograd as workers, under the most primitive conditions, produced eighteen thousand tanks, almost fifty thousand tank diesel engines, and more than seventeen million units of ammunition. And with the Cold War, Stalin would choose this region to develop his secret nuclear weapons program.

■

A military-industrial-nuclear stronghold, Chelyabinsk was closed to all foreigners, and with this came both prestige and isolation. The death of Stalin in 1953 brought the beginning of a semblance of stability: an end to the terror, and eventually a diminished fear of nighttime disappearances and hunger. Living conditions—many workers had lived in little more than underground dugouts or crowded communal barracks—improved. The Soviets developed nuclear weapons to counter the United States. They sent the first man into space. The country was at long last at peace, though a cold peace. The Kremlin promised "to catch up to and overtake" the West. But gradually stagnation set in as the cost of inefficient enterprises, lack of incentive, and the Soviet Empire and its proxies like Afghanistan drained the coffers. By the end of the 1980s, it was clear the country was close to bankrupt. Hunger was once again becoming a real fear. The Soviet leader Mikhail Gorbachev wrestled with the challenges, but his offers of growing "openness," public demonstrations, a freer press, and freer elections were not enough to keep the Soviet Union together. His biggest challenger was Boris Yeltsin, the newly elected president of Russia, one of the Soviet Union's constituent republics. In 1990, Yeltsin conspired in secret with his Ukrainian and Belorussian counterparts to replace the U.S.S.R. with a loose and powerless commonwealth.

What happened then, and next, is in many ways at the heart of today's crisis with the West. While many in the West celebrated the end of the Soviet Union, most of the fifteen member republics, including Russia, were not prepared to take advantage of the freedoms and economic challenges they unexpectedly acquired as newly independent countries. Boris Yeltsin and the "liberals" who took the reins of government in Russia were unable to resist the lure of getting rich quickly by corrupt methods. While many Western-supported NGOs promoted valuable programs and the engagement of civil society, foreigners were ultimately blamed for protecting and encouraging corrupt officials. Russians came to believe that they were seeking to undermine the country.

All this thinking remains prevalent—as a visit with Irina reminds me. In such a big country, she says, democracy is not always good; excessive freedom will lead to anarchy. She wants the Russian Orthodox Church to exert its influence as a paternalistic, unifying, and patriotic force. What the region's significant Muslim population might make of this is not something she worries about, though she has a somewhat romantic idea that the country's many ethnic groups lived happily together in the Soviet past.

President Putin has played to people like her. In 2014, his takeover of Crimea, and subsequent defense of Russian speakers in Ukraine, raised his flagging popularity rating to a whopping 80-plus percent. He has trumpeted Russian moral superiority over Western individualism, degradation, and duplicity. When it's useful, he has seconded the Orthodox Church's claims to be the one true faith and a source of Russian greatness. He has called for a universal secondary school history textbook "free of internal contradictions and ambiguities"—a challenge given any country's

history, and especially Russia's. As I write, the convened committee has failed to come up with an approved text.

Alexandr Fokin, a young history professor at Chelyabinsk
State University, says there is a demand for academics to identify
Russia's unique traits, emphasizing only the good. He says this is
both an impossible task and a perversion of history. Nonetheless,
nationalists and so-called patriots exert an influence on what he
can research and what he can say in the classroom. Chelyabinsk
is not yet as bad as the neighboring city of Yekaterinburg, where
the youth wing of Putin's United Russia party has publicly named
professors it deems traitorous. Instead, there are merely anony-
mous attacks on the Internet against those at Chelyabinsk's
universities who dare to challenge the government.

The Federal Security Service is seeking to redefine the concept of high treason to include "providing financial, technical,
advisory or other assistance to a foreign state or international
organizations, directed at harming Russia's security." In advance
of an international conference, Fokin was told by his university
that he must sign a document confirming his refusal to share secrets with his foreign colleagues, even though what constitutes a
secret now is anybody's guess. The university form included an
order that participants not reveal anything that might "inflict casualties on Russia." His sarcastic post about this on Facebook led
with "My motherland has once again reduced me to joy." The re-
sponses from fellow academics around the country reflected similar concerns—with many saying "welcome back to the U.S.S.R."

Access to government archives is getting much more difficult,
with officials saying it's best not to raise uncomfortable questions. Files that were opened in the 1990s, in the heyday of "openness," have been closed. Obtaining access to now-sensitive files is
not possible without special permission, and when that permission
is granted, it may include a restriction on foreign travel, a restriction many wish to avoid.

Foreign researchers have even greater problems, of course,

with clearance now required from the country's security services. Luckily, I met with several local historians and archivists
before this total clampdown. Were I to try to meet them now, they
say, with great regret, they would have no choice but to say no.

While Russian suspicions of the West are often unfounded
as well as cynically manipulated by the government, they are not
without foundation. Back in 1992, President George H. W. Bush
declared in his State of the Union address that "by the grace of
God America won the Cold War." But Jack Matlock, the American ambassador during the breakup of the Soviet Union, argues
that the end of the Cold War was no victory; it was a delicately
negotiated agreement that was supposed to benefit all sides and
guarantee future cooperation. According to Matlock, the United
States has all too often treated the new Russia as a loser, foment-
ing feelings of humiliation and revenge. Though no Putin apolo-
gist, he dares to argue that a lack of understanding of Russia and
Russians could unnecessarily lead to a frigid cold war and a
resumption of a nuclear arms race.

There was never any concrete promise that the West would
not expand NATO, but there was a pledge not to take advantage
of Russia's weakness. Since then, Russians believe the United
States, in particular, has done just that. The litany of Russian
concerns include NATO's expansion into Eastern Europe when
there was no longer a Cold War. Then there was NATO's bombing of Serbia, a fellow Slav and Orthodox country, without UN
Security Council approval; the approval of Kosovo's independence from Serbia despite U.S. support for maintaining territorial
sovereignty in other instances; and the U.S. withdrawal from the
Anti-Ballistic Missile Treaty and threats to station missile defenses
in former Warsaw Pact countries. Russians also cite the invasion
of Iraq without UN Security Council approval; America's participation in what they see as spurious democratic revolutions
in Ukraine, Georgia, and Kyrgyzstan; and talk of expanding
NATO to Georgia and Ukraine, both of which border Russia.

Plenty of people in the West, and some in Russia, dispute all this and say the real problem is that Moscow is becoming increasingly totalitarian and returning to its former dreams of empire. Given Russia's economic challenges and failure to modernize, they argue, Putin is seeking out enemies abroad to cover up problems at home.

In 2014, Putin found the enemies he was looking for. After the U.S.-backed Ukrainian opposition overthrew the country's pro-Russian president, tensions rose. The Ukrainian parliament passed a law that would rescind the Russian language's official status, and while the act was vetoed, Putin was already geared up to destabilize the new government.

First, he annexed the Crimea, a historically Russian peninsula jutting out into the Black Sea that had been transferred to Ukraine in 1954. When Russia and Ukraine were part of one country, that move was largely symbolic, but once they parted ways, the status of Crimea rankled. The strategically critical Crimea has an overwhelming Russian population. Moscow was forced to rent facilities for its Black Sea Fleet, with the constant threat the lease would be revoked. This became a simmering flash point, and when Russia perceived that Kiev had become less sympathetic to its interests, with U.S. support, it acted quickly. After taking over the Crimea, Putin began sending weapons and troops to support Russian speakers in Ukraine's industrial east who were looking for greater autonomy or secession.

I immediately received impassioned e-mails from contacts in Chelyabinsk, the majority of whom deplored Western sanctions and supported Putin. Many have relatives in eastern Ukraine who work in factories and mines totally dependent on the Russian market. These relatives were panicked that a Ukrainian move toward Europe would leave their family members economically and culturally stranded.

Those who came to Putin's support, especially on the takeover of Crimea, composed a surprising range of people, including some who once called themselves "the opposition." A member of the local elite I'll call V is much more pragmatic than ferocious Russian nationalists like Irina Korsunova. He says yes to Crimea. Though he deems Putin's interference in eastern Ukraine a disaster, he blames both Putin and President Obama for setting the fire. In his view, the United States acted stupidly when it interfered in Ukraine without a nuanced approach and without any attention to how loaded the situation was. As he sees it, the United States supported a coup against an elected president. The president in question might have been corrupt and despicable, but such an action only strengthens the perception that the United States applies one law to itself and another to everyone else. He says the United States needs to understand that Ukraine is of "existential importance" to Russia. It's also clear to him Ukraine cannot have a healthy economy without Russia, another thing he says the United States has failed to comprehend. "Is the West really ready to bankroll a corrupt, broken country?" he asks. He is frustrated by both sides' failure to seek a diplomatic solution to the crisis. Like the majority of Russians, he argues the impasse came about at least in part because the United States has perpetuated a security system in Europe that is based on the long-ago outcome of World War II, unnecessarily isolates Russia, and no longer fits today's world. Well versed in current events in the United States, where his children study, and an admirer of much that he sees in the United States, he is still struck by American ignorance and arrogance, bristling at Washington's readiness to condemn Russia for the same sins he believes America is known to commit.

The views of V in an upscale restaurant and of Irina Korsunova in her magazine office are reinforced amid the heat of forges and furnaces. Yura Kovach is the employee of a steel plant in Chelyabinsk and a friend for more than two decades, though his growing support for Putin has sometimes strained our relationship. We met through his wife, Irina, a frustrated Soviet economist who initially flourished in the 1990s. She created an early stock fund that would also protect pensioners; she organized a group of metalworkers who subsequently got lucrative contracts making decorative railings and banisters for new buildings. She made money while her husband, a skilled engineer, made nothing. It caused marital problems. She later scrapped her businesses and became a psychologist, burned out, and then stayed home to take care of her dying mother for several years. Along the way, she became a devoted student of an Indian guru and his meditation techniques. She became a vegetarian and started and lost a soy-tofu business—not through lack of demand, but because of government property manipulations. She then went into currency trading to try to cover her debts. Their forty-year marriage has been severely tested; their lifestyles have diverged, but they have stayed together and agree on one thing—that Vladimir Putin is the best leader for Russia. Yura has watched as his profession has lost ground to new bankers, traders, and PR specialists. He applauded when Putin called Moscow's protesters in 2010–2012 "nothing but office plankton." He introduced me to a popular working-class bard called Igor Rasteryaev, who calls NATO "trash" and extols those "who don't eat sushi or go to tanning salons." The Kovach family doesn't go out to dinner and doesn't go on foreign vacations.

Yura, who scans the Internet for news, believes the U.S. government and NGOs backed anti-Putin demonstrations in Moscow as well as the opposition protesters in Ukraine. He cannot believe the United States would allow comparable Russian interference in its own affairs or in its sphere of interest. Like so many, he now says the United States has one law for itself and another for Russia when it defends its national interests.

When I ask if there is one law for Putin and his coterie of corrupt oligarchs and another for the rest of the country, he finds excuses. He says there is corruption everywhere, ignoring Russia's international listing as one of the most corrupt countries. He stands by Putin as smart and capable, a man who will restore the country's industry and its international standing. He deflects whatever criticism of Putin I throw at him, concluding with a Russian proverb: "When there is a fire, you don't ask who the fireman is."

FOUR

THE TAXI DRIVER

I first came across Kolya outside the Chelyabinsk Opera House. The building is a modest copy of Moscow's Bolshoi, which the Soviets replicated in cities across the country. There was an openness about him that, combined with his sparkly blue eyes and gap-toothed smile, suggested he might be "my guy." Working as an illegal taxi driver, this then-thirty-year-old was parked in a prime spot for which he paid a monthly "cover charge" of fifty dollars to a local gang so the police wouldn't bother him. That proved to work only some of the time. His rusting red Zhiguli was by far the least impressive vehicle, and Kolya, in his tracksuit, was among the least well turned out, but you go by your gut, and you don't have a lot of time to deliberate. As every journalist will tell you, choosing the right driver is key. He saves your life in danger zones and is an essential guide under less stressful circumstances. Despite the car, my instincts were right. Kolya turned out to be an excellent driver in a city where the number of accidents is staggering. Residents attribute the scary statistics to more than alcohol: aggression, icy conditions, poor roads that must accommodate an ever-growing number of cars, and an explosion in the number of women drivers. On any given day, just looking out my apartment window, I would see an average of five fender benders or much worse. They rarely involved women drivers.

In addition to his driving skills, Kolya is extraordinarily street-smart. He knows Chelyabinsk inside and out, from high to low. A cousin of his owns the best restaurant, where the region's politicians gather for lunch. An uncle has made a fortune "somehow" and lives in one of the new town houses; he is also a member of the regional legislature. Kolya's clientele included a curator at a nearby museum he thought I would like to meet, and she has become one of my closest friends.

Kolya also has a history in Chelyabinsk's rougher neighborhoods. We've trolled a seemingly deserted strip where some of the city's hookers hang out. To ward off the cold and undesirables, they wait in taxis. Their stories echo those from around the globe—an abusive home life, often in a remote village or town, a desperation to get out, a tough life on the streets, pimps, a dream that it will all end one day, and fear it won't end happily.

Kolya can also ferret out the city's scuzzy and illegal underground gambling dens. He plays the slots so quickly I can't follow, though he insists his real playing days are in his past. And his past is a mess, not unusual for his generation. His mother, Tatiana, calls him "one of the lost kids of the 1990s." She says she too was lost for a while as everything she knew and grew up with dissolved. She married young to get away from alcoholic parents and worked as a cashier in a grocery store. She had Kolya in 1982, when she was eighteen. As spiraling inflation and food shortages took over in the late 1980s and early 1990s, Russians could obtain basic food items only if they had ration tickets and waited in long lines, and only then if they were lucky. Embarrassed now to admit it, Tatiana says she stole supplies from the store where she worked to sell on the black market. It was the only way to survive. Her husband, in turn, traded in illegal vodka. The family expanded to include Kolya's younger sister, and soon everyone was crammed into a two-room apartment in a former barracks, one of the many shoddy two-story structures built to house Chelyabinsk's wartime workforce. The building was long ago condemned, but it was never torn down, because housing was in great demand. Tatiana's marriage broke up. Her husband took one room and then sold it, leaving the other for her and the children. The kitchen and bathroom became communal space. It was grim.

Tatiana says Kolya was smart and engaging as a kid but a real handful. His father was absent, and she was working long hours. Kolya was largely cared for by his alcoholic grandmother. Tatiana says he was "needy" and sought out older boys whose esteem he desired. By fourteen, he was in one of the all-too-prevalent gangs, extorting from stores, providing "protection," and stealing. Tatiana says she initially had no idea what he was up to. He was in a new world she knew nothing about: "All the values I had grown up with—the Communist Party, the Communist Youth League, conformity, and the value of education—were suddenly condemned and eclipsed by quick money, the lure of luxury, and rampant crime. I had no way to guide him, no ready arguments. I was as confused as he was."

As a teenager, Kolya started sniffing glue, before moving on to the harder drugs that were suddenly flooding the city. He stole anything of value from their one room. He wormed his way into the office where Tatiana was working as a bookkeeper and broke into the company safe.

At age eighteen, Kolya was sent to a prison for first offenders for two years. The prison authorities demanded "humanitarian assistance" from Tatiana if she wanted to make sure he was not beaten. She regularly delivered building materials that she could ill afford in the hope these payoffs would also get Kolya early release. She went deep into debt to protect him.

When Kolya left prison, he resumed his drug habit, knocked up his girlfriend, and started stealing again. He took out newly available bank loans, racking up a huge debt that he will never be able to repay. He will never be able to get a bank loan again.

And under Russian law, which bans those with certain debts from leaving the country, he will never be able to travel abroad. Given his lack of education and his prison record, his job prospects are limited.

Caught stealing cell phones, Kolya was quickly convicted again. As a repeat offender, he was sent to a strict penal colony in Omsk, Siberia, far from Chelyabinsk. Tatiana could not afford to visit him. Nor could she afford to pay off the authorities while also helping support Kolya's son, her new grandson, a child incidentally Kolya has never been allowed to see. She opted for her grandchild. Kolya was furious and frightened, but he and his mother now say Omsk might have saved them both. Kolya says he was forced to behave, stopped using drugs, and promised himself he would never end up in prison again. Tatiana says, "I was finally able to breathe for the first time in years. Before Kolya was arrested the last time, I would come home wondering what hell awaited me."

At one point, when she was in total despair, Tatiana started attending New Life, a fundamentalist Baptist church that had opened in Chelyabinsk. She remarried. She has since taken courses with Lifespring, an offshoot of est that an American introduced to Chelyabinsk. Tatiana laughs, recalling that when she was in the midst of training and somewhat exhilarated, Kolya looked at her in horror, convinced she too had started drinking or taking drugs. She says Lifespring helped boost her self-esteem. She has since moved on to regular exercise classes and will soon be entering her fifties trim, attractive, and confident.

She remains close to her sister, who nonetheless lives in another world. Married to a local official, the sister is wealthy, dresses in designer labels, and travels widely, something the two could never have imagined as poor Soviet teenagers, indeed the poorest on the block. In 2014, Tatiana was still living in the condemned barracks, though she could afford to rent back the second room. Life for the past fifteen years has been stable. Her daughter manages one of the city's finest restaurants, supporting herself while finishing college. Tatiana works for a boss she calls "diligent and honest," and she is saving money to move to a new apartment.

When Kolya was released from his second round in prison, Tatiana took him to the New Life Baptist Church. It had one of the few programs in the area that assisted newly released prisoners and drug addicts. The church helped Kolya get construction work in a village that was a healthy distance away from his former friends and associates. There he met a woman named Anna. Tatiana says she can rest easier now that they are together.

When I first met Anna, she was in her mid-twenties. Slim, with long dark hair, she was gregarious, and unlike many Russians, quick to smile. She grew up in the remnants of a state farm, feeding the family's animals before heading off to school in the morning and cooking for the family when she returned in the evening. Her mother was dying of cancer. By the time Anna finished high school, the state farm, like most others, had all but collapsed, leaving hundreds unemployed.

Shock therapy, advocated by the West to replace the Soviet economic system, was most shocking in the countryside. In the 1920s and 1930s, the Soviets destroyed private farms, forcing peasants into collective and state farms. Now the post-Soviet government suddenly reversed course, telling the country's farmworkers, "You're on your own now." Cut off from state orders, state supplies, and state subsidies, the farms could not buy seeds and fertilizers. There was no feed, resulting in the wholesale slaughter of herds. The number of dairy cows dropped by 75 percent in the 1990s. As farms fell apart, the land was either stolen by crafty managers or redivided among the ill-prepared workers. With no infrastructure to back them, most couldn't make it on their own. There were no hardware stores, no spare parts for what little equipment was left, and no way to buy new tractors. Savings were eaten by spiraling inflation. Interest rates in the 1990s raged at 260 percent for those who could get loans, and farmers trying to set up new enterprises were generally considered too risky.

Some in Anna's village got jobs in trucking or construction. Anna went to work for a department store forty miles away in Chelyabinsk, a long bus ride. Her father and brother couldn't adjust and have eked out a living as seasonal laborers, harvesting potatoes for an agricultural research station. The only thing Anna and her family took away from the debris of the Soviet Union was a part of a house they were able to privatize and eventually own. It's a small cement one-story, two-family structure, immediately recognizable across the breadth of Russia as a "state farmhouse." When Kolya first took me to visit in 2012, eight family members were crammed into three small rooms: Kolya and Anna in one; Anna's brother, his wife, and two small children in another; and Anna's father and his live-in partner in the third. Kids' toys and an assortment of footwear cluttered the entryway.

To minimize dirt, the members of every Russian household must trade their shoes for slippers at the front door, a habit I have alas failed to instill at home. Sheets, towels, and clothing hung from lines in the narrow hallway to dry. Wallpaper was peeling. The floors were covered in cracked linoleum. There was no working indoor bathroom. Relations among all the family members were tense. Kolya and Anna were the only ones bringing in regular money, and they were sick of paying everyone else's vodka bills. They dreamed of building their own house on the patch of land in the back where the family grew vegetables to tide them over through the winter, at least when the regular droughts didn't kill the crops off.

To this day, the village roads are unpaved, with the odd pig, cow, or goose meandering around. Some residents still keep livestock for their own consumption, but the skeletons of barns are the only hint that not so long ago this was a farming community. The village now has gas heat, which is conveyed by aboveground pipes that line the roads like a circuitous jungle gym, rising up above junctions so that cars can pass underneath. Though it is far from picturesque, no one is complaining: the pipes represent a vast improvement over the constant scramble for wood to feed stoves. But wood still remains a necessity for the *banya*, the traditional Russian sauna one finds in most every yard. When the sewage system goes kaput, as it did on my first visit, the *banya* is not just a pleasure but a necessity. And so, when local state foresters aren't looking, the villagers head to neighboring birch groves for their supply of illegal wood. As Kolya describes the mysteries of village life, an elderly, somewhat inebriated couple emerge from the trees dragging a cart filled with logs and a gas-driven saw.

Though Anna's family house had changed not at all in the post-Soviet period, the rest of the village was alive with the hum of home improvement. The emerging haves and have-nots were now abutting one another. This is becoming a bedroom community for neighboring towns and the city. Some of the once-identical cement houses have been torn down in favor of the redbrick McMansions replete with towers and turrets, the particular taste of the late 1990s. More modest additions include vinyl siding and additional floors—the "Finnish look." People have replaced their inefficient, leaky Soviet windows with new ones. Ferocious guard dogs chained behind newly constructed fences and gates are another common denominator. Everyone is afraid of theft.

In 2013, a year later, I noticed more improvements, even to Anna and Kolya's house. The extended family had finally redone the inside, thanks in part to a government subsidy Anna's brother received for having a second child. By law, it had to be used for home renovation. The family, urged on by Kolya, did the work. No more cracked linoleum and peeling walls. The bathroom and kitchen were cleaned up and the sewage system repaired. In their spruced-up room, Kolya and Anna had a new flat-screen TV and laptop on which they watched easily downloaded pirated American movies and constant reruns of their wedding videos.

Their wedding remains a joyous memory, one they revisit

again and again. They were married in a brisk civil ceremony, but not before a series of village rituals had taken place. Kolya, looking strikingly handsome if distinctly uncomfortable in a new suit, appeared at the village house with the bouquet, accompanied by his family and Anna's closest friends. Between ribald songs, they put Kolya through a series of tests. He had to eat several slices of lemon, enduring the sour taste until he found his bride's name under one of them. There were several questions about Anna's height, weight, and waist size to be answered, with a fine if he muffed it. Kolya had to choose the right-sized shoes for her from three pairs he was offered. To finally gain access to her, he then had to drink a huge jar of homemade juice at the bottom of which was the key to the house and his new life. That was the last nonalcoholic beverage to be seen for many days. At last, Anna appeared in a stunning strapless wedding dress. Kolya's mother presented the couple with an icon.

Accompanied by their friends and large quantities of champagne, the couple drove into the city and walked around Chelyabinsk, stopping at the requisite sites—the Tomb of the Unknown Soldier and the sculpture of a beggar whose pate they touched for luck. At the banquet in a local restaurant, Kolya's mother welcomed them again, this time with bread and salt, a traditional greeting signifying hospitality and long life. From then on, the proceedings got more and more raucous with toasts, chants of "bitter, bitter," which led the newlyweds to sweeten the atmosphere with endless kissing, and wild dancing. But that wasn't the end of the celebrations. Hungover guests engaged in two more days of feasting and drinking in the nearby woods. The men dressed as women and the women as men, a tradition for which I found no explanation but much glee. Meat was barbecued. Gallons of home brew, long in preparation, were consumed, and several trips to the local liquor store were made to replenish the depleted stocks with vodka.

Though the house was now redone, tensions remained. Anna

and Kolya were still the only ones with regular jobs, and they worked long hours. Kolya did the overnight shift from Thursday through Saturday, ferrying around the Chelyabinsk club crowd, who by the early hours had more money than sense. His customers were often so drunk they paid him several times over. "I don't steal from them; they steal from themselves," he says, laughing, "paying me double, sometimes treble." Kolya recalls giving a break to one customer who asked to be driven to various addresses across the city. He would get out, pour a shot, down it, and then get back in the red car. At some point, Kolya realized he was an Afghan War vet who was drinking to his fallen comrades. He says he didn't charge him.

It was a challenging time for the couple. To their delight, Anna was pregnant. But as employers often demand, she was paid under the table at the department store where she worked. This meant she would get only a minimal amount—sixty dollars a month— for maternity leave and her job wasn't guaranteed in the future. And then Kolya dropped the real bomb.

He hadn't been looking particularly well, and I put it down to a bout of pneumonia, but months later he still looked pretty ravaged. He came to the apartment I was renting for a cup of tea. He looked around, motioned to his ears to ask if someone was listening in, and then threw caution to the wind. "It's time for me to tell you something. I was afraid to initially, afraid what your reaction would be. I am HIV positive."

Kolya tested positive when he was first in prison in 2000. He has since refused treatment despite pleas from Anna and his immediate family, who are the only ones who know about his condition. Though he's driven me several times to the Infectious Disease Center, run by a great and sympathetic man, Kolya refuses to listen to me. "I don't believe in this therapy. I have friends who haven't done well on it. I am healthy," he insists. He says Anna is HIV negative. "I will live as long as God gives me. Don't bring this up again."

If I'd been smarter, I would have known long since. His stories about his life in prison were sometimes confused. When I pushed him on particulars, like his work detail and where he lived, nothing quite added up. The reason is now clear. In those days, HIV-positive prisoners were isolated from the rest of the population. They weren't allowed to work and were known derisively as "chocolates." Kolya was a "chocolate."

Another year passes. It's 2014. I arrive at Chelyabinsk airport, and who should be standing there at 5:00 a.m. but Kolya. He looks a lot better, and thanks to contacts he has a new job working for a limo company that caters to businesspeople visiting from Moscow. It pays relatively well. It's legal. It's not dangerous. He has access to a new Ford, which he can use in his off-hours, and he no longer has to worry about the now-dead Zhiguli or the police.

Ukraine is in the headlines, and Kolya uncharacteristically starts talking politics. Somewhat supportive of the Russian leader Vladimir Putin in the past—"the man who brought us stability"—he has now become a true fan. He gets all his news from state-funded TV stations and echoes the constant diatribes about fascists in Ukraine, a renewal of Russian pride, and the dangers of American enemies, though he quickly points out I am an exception. His once-positive view of the United States has been eclipsed. As we stop at a market to buy some supplies, he dismisses concerns about a looming economic crisis, adding that sanctions will at last force Russia to develop its domestic industries. "I am a patriot," he says as we once again head to the village. When we arrive, Anna is already rolling out dough to make traditional *pelmeni* (delicate Russian dumplings), all the while keeping an eagle eye on their ten-month-old daughter, Christina, who is propelling herself around the tiny kitchen in one of those spinning chairs on wheels. Anna begins preparing the meat filling, asking how much the ground beef cost. It's 70 percent more than just a few weeks ago. Buckwheat, a Russian staple, will shortly quadruple in price. Anna breaks in when Kolya once again extols Putin and Russian actions in Ukraine. She is bitter about the subsidies and free housing Ukrainian refugees are being offered, while young families like hers continue to struggle.

At home, tensions continue. Kolya has to keep scolding his drunk father-in-law, who constantly stumbles into the kitchen interrupting our conversation. But a few weeks later, there's good news. Kolya's mother, Tatiana, has finally succeeded in buying a new apartment. Anna and Kolya and their beautiful, chubby, healthy daughter will move into the barracks. Once in the city, in their own space, Anna hopes that Christina will have access to all the things she never had, including music lessons and a good school. The subject of Kolya's health is not to be discussed.

FIVE

A GAY LIFE

There is an active LGBT life in Chelyabinsk, though it's by no means as vibrant or as open as one might wish. As Sergei Avdeev, head of the city's youth services, described it to me a few years ago when he was still willing to speak frankly, life for individuals whose sexual orientation is nontraditional remains much as it was in the United States forty years ago, or how it perhaps still is in rural Alabama.

Ask people in Chelyabinsk if they know anyone who is gay, and they will probably say no and show discomfort at the thought. However, when pressed, they might just acknowledge they do know someone who is a bit "different." Given the overwhelmingly negative attitudes toward the LGBT community, few publicly come out, fearing family complications or discrimination at work. Even so, gay culture has emerged from the underground, and there are plenty of online sites and gay meeting places. As one gay friend put it, "There is our life, and then there is rest of the Russia."

Same-sex intercourse was illegal in the Soviet Union and remained punishable by up to five years in prison until it was finally decriminalized in 1993. Gay culture quickly gained a following in Moscow and St. Petersburg, where it was seen as a sign of the new hip and avant-garde. But when gay activists demanded more than just being a source of entertainment, the backlash followed. A Muslim leader condoned beating up gays and got away with it. The Orthodox Church denounced same-sex relationships as a sin. Right-wing lawmakers joined the charge, and several cities passed laws that banned spreading information about nontraditional sexual relations to minors. In 2013, the country's parliament followed suit. While nominally aimed at protecting children, the new national law was widely understood as an effort to suppress homosexuality and Russia's fledgling gay rights movement. Under the vague terms of the law, a gay parade can be interpreted as a criminal offense. Secondary and even university teachers I know will not go near the subject, fearful that merely talking about homosexuality, even as a literary theme, could be construed as "homosexual propaganda directed at minors."

In the run-up to the 2014 Sochi Winter Olympics, when Russia's growing homophobia became a public relations nightmare for the International Olympic Committee and the Russian organizers, President Putin said the law does not impose sanctions against homosexuality, adding, "The law does not in any way infringe on the rights of sexual minorities. They are full-fledged members of our society and are not being discriminated against in any way."

The reality is quite different. When Putin speaks of Russia's moral superiority over the West, it is clear to most Russians that he is also attacking homosexuality. Countries that allow same-sex marriages or unions have been banned from adopting Russian children. To reinforce the point, Putin appointed a raging, vocal homophobe to head the nation's propaganda machine.

Dmitry Kiselyov, the most powerful man in Russian media, not only declared publicly that gays should be prohibited from donating organs but added that their hearts, upon death, should be burned or buried because they are "unsuitable for extending the life of another." His diatribes were not limited to the dignity of dead homosexuals. Kiselyov went on to blame a twenty-two-year-old Russian man for bringing about his own brutal murder because his open homosexuality had provoked his assailants. No one suggested Kiselyov's remarks had violated Russia's laws against hate speech.

The new laws and the prominence of people like Kiselyov have emboldened violent antigay activists. When some gay people protested the propaganda law by kissing outside the State Duma, the lower house of parliament, police officers stood by and watched as the demonstrators were doused with water and beaten.

Georgy, a thirty-year-old gay man in Chelyabinsk, has been quietly dropped from the meetings of the region's youth council he used to attend. He has never come out publicly, but his long boots and tight jeans, not your usual Chelyabinsk menswear, as well as his distinctive mannerisms, were enough to raise suspicions and sufficient for him to be shunned by the youth organization. However, he is a skilled public relations and sales manager and has no trouble finding work.

As homophobia became more pronounced, Georgy became more cautious about using gay social network sites, fearing set-ups and provocations. A friend who went to an apartment after meeting someone online was beaten up and forced to name other gay people in the city. He was outed, lost his job, and has fled Chelyabinsk.

Georgy now has a partner, but they are discreet. While a very few friends who work in the theater might dare to hold hands in public, he laughs at the idea. Gay demonstrations in the city have occurred, but they too have been discreet, so much so that many people passing by probably had no idea what was going on. At their height, before the 2013 law, perhaps a hundred would gather and let off multicolored balloons, saying nothing. It was a quiet, defiant stand by the members of the gay community and their families and friends. Perhaps half that number might gather annually now. Gays debate to what degree Western attention and public demonstrations have helped or hurt them.

The most popular gay meeting place in town is called Neon,

which is run by Ludmilla Abramzon. Once married, with a young child, she is now an avowed lesbian with a partner. Her Facebook page hides little, but when she needs to—when she's dealing with her daughter's school or catering for straight events—she can appear straight or "natural," the word even Russian gays use. But come midnight on Fridays, Saturdays, and Sundays, Neon turns into a classy, outrageously camp gay club. One weekend night when I was there, a straight wedding wrapped up late as the gay crowd arrived. I can't believe the wedding party didn't know Neon's full repertoire, given its splashy photographs on the Web, but there was nonetheless a scramble to make sure the two groups should not meet.

Taxi drivers certainly know the club's reputation, and when given the address, they will often demand the client sit in the back of their cabs, as though homosexuality were a contagious disease. At the entrance, Ludmilla's team of bouncers screen those wishing to come in so skinheads or other "provocateurs" don't make trouble. They check bags, looking for evidence of drugs. The last thing Ludmilla needs is a police raid, and so far the club has not been hassled by police or local authorities. She jokes it may be the cleanest bar in town. Ludmilla usually sits in a side room scanning closed-circuit monitors to ensure nothing gets out of hand. The cabaret, featuring drag queens, goes on until dawn. The performances are deliciously clever, full of parodies, racy double entendres, and audience participation. Even though I am relatively fluent in Russian, I had to regularly consult my dictionary, which alas did not help.

While sitting there on many a night, I got to know several of the denizens: young male lawyers, accountants, and IT mavens who would never dare come out and jeopardize their jobs and who described the well-known hardships of growing up in a society that is largely intolerant of anyone who is "different." Unlike many Russian men, they are strikingly lean and good-looking; they attribute this to the competition among gay men in Chelyabinsk to find a partner. "Natural" men, they say, can let themselves go and still get by.

One of Ludmilla's dancers, Sasha, is androgynous, a young man with budding breasts and feminine hips but with all his male equipment. We almost didn't meet, because I was waiting outside a café for a young man, and Sasha, with well-cut shoulder-length hair and a hint of makeup, could easily pass for a woman. After a certain amount of confusion and cell phone calls, we finally found each other. Sasha says his position is even more complicated than most because gay men are afraid to be seen with him publicly for fear Sasha will draw unwanted attention. He says the government's antigay legislation creates the impression that all homosexuals are pedophiles. Sasha scoffs at the pervasive fear that "naturals" are going to turn gay should they be exposed to more information. After a lonely, confused, and tortured adolescence, he says the absence of counseling for young gay men and women, now essentially banned by law, is cruel. He thinks about leaving the country, and he has a chance because his father, who long ago abandoned the family, was an American citizen. Still, Sasha has found a community in Chelyabinsk of friends and support and is loath to leave what he believes is his home.

But it's a home that has defied changes that have taken place in the West, becoming less, not more, tolerant in recent years. Sasha can't imagine gay marriage being accepted here in his lifetime, and he sees the prospects for gays to have families only getting worse. A gay couple who slipped through the cracks and managed to adopt a few years ago tells me they could never expect to do so now. They worry that social services could take away their child at any moment. Several young same-sex couples I have met are now thinking about trying to emigrate so that they can one day have families.

Vika, a close friend of Ludmilla's and a sister lesbian, is as rotund and unfortunately attired as Ludmilla is lithe and sophisticated. Having made it from nothing as a teenage single mother, she is approaching thirty with a generous if no-bullshit attitude. She describes being the daughter of a "bandit" who ran protection rackets in Chelyabinsk's Gagarin Park. Eventually, her father lost everything and joined a "sect" where he still lives entirely off the grid with no electricity or running water. Her parents divorced. She went wild and ran away with a gypsy until her father's associates threatened him. Her gypsy love eventually died young of a drug overdose. Vika meanwhile had his child and kept it.

After a few years working in a factory, she came across a community of lesbians who met in a Chelyabinsk courtyard. She's since had female partners and would like another who is as strong as she is. She broke free from the factory, worked as a courier, and saw some business openings. She now has a successful company organizing kids' parties. While doing volunteer work in an orphanage, she came across a malnourished, abandoned child. With the agreement of the staff, who realized the child needed a real home, she fostered the little girl, who became a member of her family. When the birth mother reappeared, still on drugs and with no means of support, the court heard testimony that Vika was a lesbian. Parental rights are readily revoked in Russia, but the mother's drug issues and physical abuse of her young child were considered less heinous than Vika's sexual orientation. Vika anticipates the birth mother will once again abandon the child, and she keeps tabs—waiting for her moment.

She hides her sexual orientation from her twelve-year-old son lest he be tortured at school. Her relatives, who turn to her for financial support and admire her brains and business success, have refused to acknowledge her female partners. "They all ask when I am getting married," she says ruefully. However, she says, "It's easier to be a lesbian than a gay guy, since everyone just thinks this is a phase and I just need to meet the right man."

SIX

THE RUSSIAN FAMILY

It's 2013. Dima and Tatiana's large kitchen opens onto a spacious two-story living room full of teenagers and toddlers, strollers and toys. It's a Saturday night, not long before the New Year's holiday, and a group of Chelyabinsk's well-heeled families have gathered in one of the city's upscale gated communities to make dinner together. While they enjoy an excellent selection of fine wines, vodka, and hors d'oeuvres, the conversation jumps from discussions of the best ski resorts in Europe and the United States and where to go for their next vacation to where they should send their children to school overseas.

Tatiana rolls out dough to make *pelmeni*. One guest, back from a hunting trip, has provided venison for the filling. Another friend, the owner of a successful restaurant, where the city's movers and shakers are regularly to be found, has provided ground beef and fish. After everyone pitches in to fill and pinch dozens of stuffed dough triangles, talking all the while about yoga classes, someone's latest trip to Antarctica, and the comparative merits of U.S. versus Russian education, the restaurant owner takes over. He tosses the *pelmeni* into boiling water scented with garlic and bay leaves and prepares a butter-garlic sauce.

Now in their late thirties and their forties, these couples are success stories. They have started trading companies and construction businesses. One is well placed in the local government. They have all traveled widely and often; the chef and his wife lived and trained in Spain and plan to go back there again for six months, leaving their restaurant in the hands of trusted staff. Others are lured by the winter warmth of Miami, a popular resort for Russians.

They all now have large houses in Chelyabinsk's new suburbs, with space to accommodate growing families. After having one child in their early twenties, when they were still struggling, one couple now has four more after a gap of several years. Dima and Tatiana have two teenagers and two under two. On the surface, this would appear to be Putin's dream: expanding, stable Russian families. There is one catch. Tatiana spent months in Miami to ensure her last two could be born in the United States. An agency there arranges everything, including translators for the birth.

While still based in Russia, the family has insured themselves and their children against an uncertain future. The two older children, born when their parents had not yet made enough money to travel, do not have foreign citizenship, but they are now studying in London and the United States so they can go to the best colleges abroad.

On that evening in 2013, these families were happy to come and go and didn't blink at private school tuition in the United States and England of fifty thousand dollars a year. But a year later, the "uncertain future" they feared is becoming a reality. Some are now exploring ways to shift their money and families permanently out of the country while they are still young enough to start over.

While New York and especially European cities have long attracted Russia's superrich, the growing number of middle-class business owners who are now exiting the country is an ominous development for the Russian economy. Small and medium-sized enterprises make up only around a quarter of Russia's economy, a smaller proportion than in most economies, but they are a crucial part of the government's plan to wean the country off imports.

The problem of capital flight is matched by concern about brain drain in a country still struggling with a demographic crisis. When the Soviet Union broke apart, Russia was left with a tiny population to control a vast landmass. While there are more than 300 million Americans, Russia has a mere 142 million in a country almost twice the size. With the economic hardships of the 1990s, the population declined by a million a year because of falling birthrates, plummeting life expectancy, and unusually high emigration rates. With the drop off the demographic cliff, experts feared that the population could fall by 30 percent by 2050. Those predictions have proved overly pessimistic thanks to a decade of relative economic stability, government subsidies, and government messages. President Putin declared a holiday to give couples time off to make babies, and on one Valentine's Day he urged couples to do their patriotic duty and procreate. Birthrates have finally increased modestly. In 2012, post-Soviet Russia registered its first natural population growth. But the country still faces huge problems in funding its pension system, filling the military draft, and creating a future workforce. The loss of families like Dima and Tatiana's would be a huge blow.

In addition to increasing the birthrate, Russian officials hope to attract immigrants over the coming years to avoid labor shortages. But they don't want just any immigrant. Putin has urged Russians who live in the former Soviet states to move, but the largest number of immigrants are coming from the impoverished South Caucasus and central Asia. They are people many Russians disparagingly call "blacks."

While I was being questioned by Russian migration officials, they openly expressed their disgust with the "pollution" of their country by non-Slavic immigrants. Though Russian state TV has made a propaganda point out of U.S. racism, it has also aired programs about the negative results of ethnic diversity in America. The Russian migration officials were certain that I too would be upset about the growing numbers of Hispanics in my country. They launched into a diatribe about the similar situation in Russia, comparing Hispanic immigrants to the "unwashed heathen from central Asia who should never set foot in Holy Russia."

To encourage the domestic birthrate, the government has implemented numerous programs. Maternity leave is now among the most generous in the world: 140 days at full salary, paid for by the employer, followed by a government subsidy worth 40 percent of the woman's salary for three years while a woman stays at home. Parents also get a lump-sum payment for each child born after the first, a further incentive to have bigger families. A woman's job is guaranteed for two years after birth.

It looks great, but the reality is not always quite so rosy. Women's salaries still lag way behind men's, so, as one woman put it, "forty percent of nothing is nothing." And there's another Russian twist. Like Kolya's wife, Anna, many women are forced to work off the books so their employer won't have to pay maternity leave and social security taxes. Such an arrangement leaves women with only a tiny maternal leave stipend and no job security. It is common for employers to put gender and age requirements in their want ads so they can weed out prospective mothers. Labor laws need changing. Paternity leave is an unexplored, unaccepted concept.

Natalia Baskova, a member of the Chelyabinsk city council and head of the region's family welfare committee, created an almighty storm when she said her dream was that Russian women be required to marry and have a child by age twenty while they are healthy and fertile. Because Russia's minorities often do this by tradition, she was clearly speaking about increasing the ethnic Russian population. As it turned out, her dream was many women's nightmare.

The Internet went wild with outraged comments demanding her resignation or better still her head. Women filed angry posts, saying they were not going to return to Soviet days, when couples married young, had a child, and lived with their parents in a one- or two-room apartment while struggling to finish their education and maintain their sanity. Other furious respondents said couples now need a solid education and financial base before starting a successful marriage. They complained of low salaries, the exorbitant cost of housing, and the illegal payments demanded for so-called free education and medical treatment. They decried the closure of state day-care centers. Women again and again cited the absence of "adequate, sober partners."

Baskova quickly backed down, saying she had floated her proposal as a joke in order to stress what was truly needed to support the Russian family and increase the country's birthrate. But over a long conversation, it became clear Baskova was not joking. She worries that with more options, many Russian women, especially the more educated, are no longer ready to settle down quickly and have the children Russia desperately needs.

Her daughters' friends are in their late twenties and early thirties, and Baskova estimates only 20 percent are married. The rest are more interested in traveling, building their careers, and waiting, as she put it, "for a wealthy, decent man." She thinks they are mistaken and risk becoming so independent and spoiled they will never accept the demands and responsibilities that come with having children. She blames the new capitalism and media for promoting glamour and selfishness. For her, the bottom line is that there is no way for a woman to realize herself other than in family life.

This is not what I expected to hear. Baskova, a tiny woman barely hitting five feet, had been a towering figure in Chelyabinsk's nascent women's movement during the 1990s. With the help of foreign grants, she created an NGO to address issues like rape and family violence that had long been ignored by police and social services. She backed emerging women business owners and tried to increase the number of elected women officials, though that campaign met with little success. Somewhere along the way, she moved in a different direction and decided to focus on Russia's demographic crisis and support for families. "I recognize the right of women to have a choice, but I am not at all sure they will be happier for it, strange as it may sound from a woman in the women's rights movement."

I posed the question of women's rights and their growing choices to everyone I met. Baskova got support from Tatiana Arkhipova, the dynamic principal of School 148. After Tatiana had shown me videos and photographs documenting her students' achievements, she began to reflect on her own life. Tatiana walked out of her marriage to someone she describes as a "do-nothing" husband but now thinks she made a mistake. She says she should have shut up and stayed with the demanding man for whom she cooked and cleaned while he watched sports and wandered. She thinks young women risk being too picky for their own good. "Women are monogamous; men are by nature polygamous. It's like the farm, one bull and lots of females. So we need to teach our women to be patient and understand this. I didn't and should have."

She does not believe you can change nature. She watches the new rich parents at her school, where many of the men have had three or more wives, each one younger than the last. "The poor women," she observes. "Well, that's just the way it is. Women are in a bad position here. First, there are more women than men, and it's really hard to find a good man here given the high rates of alcoholism."

In the 1990s, Russian women were under the impression that finding a man in the West would solve their problems, and there was a brisk trade in Russian brides. Russian women thought

American men would be ideal partners, and American men anticipated grateful, sexy, yet docile stay-at-home cooks and cleaners. They were both tragically misinformed.

In 1997, dozens of women from across the country, including Chelyabinsk, turned up for a "get-together" with American men at Moscow's Rossiya Hotel. Compared with the assemblage of pretty seedy middle-aged American men, the Russian women were for the most part young, attractive, educated single mothers abandoned by drunken husbands or victims of the economic crisis. They were desperate for a "good" man and a future and were under the impression that meant Americans. I spent a lot of time in the hotel bathroom with several of the women as they wondered what they had gotten themselves into. As I left, the American organizers threw me to the ground and stamped on my recording equipment. Just why, they never said, though their anger suggested they didn't want me to report that Russian women found the American men lacking in some way. It didn't matter that this occurred in the public lobby, because the organizers, as corrupt as any Russian, had paid off the security and lobby staff. The staff did not come to my immediate aid but subsequently said how humiliated they were to see "good" Russian women trying to leave the country. The whole picture was one of American sleaze and Russian ignominy.

Alcoholism remains the bane of Russian family life, a major factor in a divorce rate that is now number one in the world. Workers on their way to the factory and kids well under the legal drinking age stroll the streets, beers in hand, not even bothering to stash them in a discreet brown paper bag. Attitudes to drinking among professionals are slowly changing for the better. The Chelyabinsk City Youth Office is encouraging sports programs and healthy living. The government has launched efforts to limit the sale of alcohol, especially beer, which until recently was readily available at every corner kiosk with no one checking IDs. But as the economy worsened in 2015, President Putin ordered his government to rein in soaring vodka prices. His explanation was made on health grounds; the rising prices, he said, would only lead to increased consumption of poisonous bootleg spirits. Of course, the price controls would also be popular and help ward off possible protests.

Over the past ten years, Russians are on average living a little longer, drinking themselves to death less frequently, killing themselves less often, and killing each other more rarely, but the statistics still aren't great in global terms. The Russian taste for liquor is still serious. Twenty-five percent of Russian men die before the age of fifty-five, compared with 7 percent in most Western countries, and researchers cite alcohol as a key reason. While women generally live to seventy-six, average life expectancy for men is only sixty-five—up slightly but well below the American figure of seventy-eight. If Baskova had her way, the state would return to Soviet norms and once again force an alcoholic husband to get treatment. "I know we talk about an individual's rights now," she says, "but what about the rights of a family?" Soviet "treatment," however, did not result in improved statistics.

Baskova no longer looks at the 1990s, with its political and economic turmoil and growing individualism, with the same enthusiasm she once felt, saying flat out, "I don't want to repeat that period. I cannot allow it. We destroyed as much as we developed." In the run-up to the last presidential elections, she panicked at growing opposition to Vladimir Putin's United Russia party, small as it was in Chelyabinsk, saying, "I saw the prospect of anarchy again, and I don't want it." Admitting that she sounds like a romantic, even a Soviet throwback, Baskova wants unity, everyone together, and she enthusiastically backed the All-Russian National Front, a movement Putin created as an electoral strategy to boost his party's ebbing support. Its stated goal was "to unite all Russians, including the unaffiliated, civic organizations and businessmen who share our values, ideas and philosophy on how to make Russia a more prosperous and great nation." It was a

Kremlin gambit to expand its leverage. Baskova, a self-declared independent, doesn't deny Kremlin manipulation of the system, but she bought in, calling it an inspiring way to get people together to solve common problems; for her, the biggest such problems are those facing families.

When Baskova "jokingly" mandated young women have children, the list of impediments thrown back at her included cuts in promised subsidies for young families, a shortage of day-care facilities, and continued cramped living conditions. Sanctions, imposed because of Russian actions in Ukraine, have exacerbated a budget crisis in Chelyabinsk and other Russian regions. And what to do about the lack of eligible men? That is a stumper. Online dating has taken off, and there are plenty of sites where Russian women still advertise for a foreign husband, though dismal reports from those who embarked on foreign marriages have dimmed that business.

Natalia Baskova prodded the local government to set up its first family crisis center, where free counseling is available to deal with domestic violence and provide assistance for dysfunctional families. There is a hotline and a roster of psychologists, though their training is poor and there aren't enough of them. Meanwhile, there is still only one small government-funded shelter for women at risk for the entire region of three million people. The staff would like to learn more about mediation techniques, and some quietly express regret about the shrinking access to foreign grants brought on by Moscow's increased xenophobia.

Changing long-established gender and behavior patterns is a long-term challenge anywhere, but this is a start. Until recently, the local government more often than not solved family problems by removing children and placing them in state orphanages, where it's now widely acknowledged children fare badly.

None of these issues are particularly new, but with the "new capitalism" they have become more pronounced, and they are now openly discussed. Russian women talk about their endurance with a mixture of pride and resentment. They say it's not for nothing Russia is the "motherland" and that the statue most often used to symbolize the country's fight for survival and salvation is a vast looming female. Women have risen to a challenge they wish they didn't face, the double burden of working and taking care of the family, often under impossible conditions.

The best place for women to talk about their lives is the Russian *banya*, or "bathhouse," by all accounts the most delicious of Russian traditions and one still shared by everyone regardless of economic status. A *banya* can be a pricey commercial enterprise replete with any number of beauty treatments, but better still is a homemade *banya* in one's own yard. Humid steam grows hotter as the expert in the group tosses water onto heated stones to regulate the temperature. The addition of oils to the stones can divert the conversation for a while as the assembled assess each oil's particular medicinal benefit. Naked women with an assortment of odd head coverings (a hat of some kind is imperative) shift in an oft-rehearsed dance to benches at different levels, depending on their tolerance for heat.

Languorous discussions are interspersed with douses of cold water, scrubbing, homemade facials, cups of tea, perhaps a beer, and the invigorating beating with birch branches. A regular topic is the relative qualities of the sexes. It's hard to find women who have much good to say about Russian men, but utter the word "feminism" and the immediate reaction is one of disgust— perhaps because women were forced to adopt a warped kind of feminism in Soviet times, without being asked if they really wanted it. The U.S.S.R. espoused the rights to equal pay and equal opportunity, though they were unfulfilled. At the same time, women were also expected to take care of the family.

While women may shun "feminism" per se, there is much discussion about the changing roles of the sexes. This is a hot topic in women's magazines, such as the Russian versions of *Cosmopolitan*, *Glamour*, and *Vogue*. Women want to be spoiled a little, it is often said. They want to be given flowers, have their coats handed to them and doors opened, but they don't want that to be an excuse for later humiliation and abuse. It's a delicate balance.

Today's Russian women typically look little like their mothers, who shuttled between work, food lines, and the kitchen and appeared old and exhausted by forty. They describe themselves as stronger, more flexible, and more cultured than men, who are often labeled brash and crass. The 1990s put added burdens on those men. Many couldn't deal with losing their jobs and their status. A friend says, "While many men took to their couch and the bottle, we women forced ourselves to adjust. Someone had to feed the children." Women engineers, doctors, and scientists swallowed their pride and looked for whatever opportunities they could to earn money.

Elena Kornilova, a former teacher, joined the hordes of Russian women shuttling to the bazaars of China and Turkey, returning to sell cheap goods in Chelyabinsk's grimy, freezing open-air markets. She became adept at playing on constantly changing exchange rates. She was a good businesswoman. Her success fed the family, but it also fueled marital problems. Her husband started drinking more, and soon after their divorce he died young of cirrhosis of the liver, leaving her with two young children. Elena survived. Dressed in leggings, her dark hair fashionably cut and nails glittering with silver polish, she has had a thriving Amway franchise for more than five years and is happy to describe her bonuses, her climb up the corporate ladder, and the free Amway trips she has earned.

The best of Russia now resides in its women, declares Roman, a devoted father of two and one of the few men in his village who has prospered. "They take responsibility for the children, and they are willing to work hard." Just over forty, he has slowly built up a business producing and supplying plastic panes for greenhouses and construction. Looking back at his high school class of seventeen boys, he starts counting: Two were murdered, two more died of unknown causes, others became petty criminals or drunks. In sum, he concludes, "There are five of us who live more or less normal family lives."

His take is that Russian men are cursed by the belief they should make a quick million or do nothing at all. "Russians are heroes by their nature and, when pushed, can do amazing things, but instead of great deeds, life now demands little ones, step by step, and Russian men are incapable of dealing with that. They don't understand that from small deeds grow bigger ones. You don't get a million without starting with ones.

"It's up to women to fix this," he believes. "Women have to save us from ourselves. They need to teach their sons. It's going to take two generations, at least forty years."

I once attended a public discussion about male-female relationships shortly ahead of Valentine's Day, a Western import that is now a popular holiday. It included a seemingly unlikely but typical pairing—a fortune-teller, testifying to the deep and enduring power of superstition, and a psychologist for the Russian Orthodox Church. The fortune-teller blamed Russian men for the failure of relationships, saying they treat women like playthings. She said 90 percent of her female clients ask for love potions. The Orthodox psychologist chastised Russian women for being too domineering, blaming their efforts to change their husbands for the breakup of marriages.

"Family values" is the ever-repeated mantra coming from President Putin, though he has himself divorced. The government and the Orthodox Church say go have more babies; economic opportunities or the lack thereof and changing social mores tell men and women something different.

When Russian families succeed, they are close, loving, supportive, and multigenerational (even if there are plenty of searing mother-in-law jokes). It's still deemed shameful not to take care of elderly parents. Irina Kovach and the school principal Tatiana Arkhipova both cared for their mothers at home for several years. Other friends visit their elderly parents daily. The idea of putting them in state-run nursing homes, just about the only ones that exist, is met with justifiable horror and shame. For generations, the pattern was much the same. Grandfathers often died young, but grandmothers remained an essential part of family life, living in and helping to care for children while the young parents finished college or went to work.

But young people are waiting longer to get married. They are now increasingly able to move out on their own and relocate to other towns or cities in search of employment opportunities. Grandmothers now have careers that engage them, or they decide to augment their tiny pensions, working well past fifty-five, the young age at which women can still retire with benefits. There is a roiling debate about increasing pension ages as the population lives longer. Family dynamics are changing.

SEVEN

STUBBORN PARENTS

When Elena Zhernova gave birth, Russian doctors, with no concrete diagnosis, said her son would never walk, talk, or respond. In the midst of postpartum confusion, she was told to give up her newborn, forget him, and have another "healthy" child. Stunning their physicians, she and her husband refused. Their son is now studying international management in college.

Russian doctors have long advised, or rather ordered, parents to hand over special-needs children to government institutions where they are fed, provided with only the most basic health care, and offered no chance for development or education. That's the way it was in the Soviet Union, and that's the way it has generally remained.

In Chelyabinsk, you might easily get the impression there are no "unusual" children, the most polite word Russians use to describe those with special needs. They are invisible. There has been little or no accommodation for those with special needs in public spaces. There are often overwhelming problems just leaving a typical Russian apartment. Elevator doors may be too narrow to fit a state-issued wheelchair, and stairs can be an insuperable obstacle.

Russians have long looked on families who defied the advice, if not outright orders, of doctors to give up their children with little understanding or compassion. Life, after all, was hard for the healthiest. Families of challenged children tell me again and again they have lived in something approximating shame or hell. Denied adequate education, their children, who have a huge range of abilities and disabilities, and often receive wrong diagnoses, have been condemned to loneliness and isolation. The prevailing view is that their children are uneducable, with no chance of being productive, integrated members of society.

According to Elena Zhernova, the state social services system still assigns children with special needs to crude "boxes," with no differentiation for the individual case. If you have Down's syndrome, you go in one box, with no anticipation of progress. If you are autistic, you go in another. If you have cerebral palsy, you are doomed to another similarly crude box. Protests by parents are typically met with stony stares and comments like "We know more than you, and you have no role."

This grim situation, which American parents have also battled and still battle, is now being challenged by some dedicated, incredibly stubborn Russian parents, who are no longer willing to give up their children or to accept isolation and a hopeless prognosis. In Chelyabinsk, Elena Zhernova is now leading the charge, inspired by others in Russia and around the world who have shown what is possible.

She started fighting for her son Nikita, whose prognosis proved to be totally wrong. A teacher by training, she dreamed up exercises and games to spur his development. At a year, he started talking. He started learning English. He began to read. His motor skills approached normal. Despite this, schools took one look at his official assessment at birth and rejected him. Refusing to take no for an answer, Elena finally persuaded one school to accept Nikita, and he thrived there. Then she began to help other parents work with their children. She received a grant from a foreign NGO to visit specialists in Poland, where she met a man who used horses as therapy for cerebral palsy patients. She came home, bought a horse, and set up her own program, hoping the therapy could be adapted to help her son and others, including young people who had been warehoused in state institutions.

■

One fall, as Nikita prepared to write the perennial back-to-school essay "What I Did on My Summer Vacation," he jokingly sniped, "What am I going to say, that I spent the time in a madhouse?" At that point, Elena revealed to him that given his original diagnosis he could have ended up in a madhouse. "I remember his eyes when I told him the truth," she says. While studying at college, he now works with challenged children in his spare time.

Once Nikita was launched, Elena had more time to focus on others, explaining, "I couldn't let them do nothing." In 2010, she met a successful businessman who had a newborn daughter with Down's syndrome. Dima had never seen a child with Down's before but refused his doctor's "suggestions" that he and his wife give her up. "I don't want to emigrate," he told Elena. "I want my daughter to have a future here. I have money to contribute."

Along with Dima and other parents, Elena put together a center called Starry Rain. The government gave them a basement warehouse. The families cleared it of trash and using their own funds, plus donations, transformed the space into a cheery modern facility. Elena is particularly proud of the bathrooms. Not only are they among the few in the city designed to accommodate those who are physically challenged, but they also feature colored tiles, with pictures of various animals. With her irrepressible sense of joy, she was determined that the center be anything but "stark, depressing, institutional." The families have seen enough of that, and she proved to be a skilled negotiator, often getting what she needed for less than cost. She charmed the builders into finishing the job in record time, and one talented mother has since painted fanciful murals on all the walls.

Led by Elena and a staff of similarly enthusiastic and creative specialists, the center offers children with a range of disabilities individual evaluations and free therapy, though the range of therapy is more limited than she would wish. More than anything, it is a place where children can socialize and where they are encouraged to develop. It's also a place where parents can share their concerns and learn how to work with their children at home. Elena tries to draw on best practices from everywhere, though the Internet can be confusing, with conflicting reports and too many promises of miracle drugs that parents are quick to glom on to. She looks for information and programs that parents can replicate. "If it's super-duper complicated, with fancy equipment, that won't work for us. We have lots of kids and need to rely on what little we have." She has organized summer camps for families with challenged children where they set up tents, share their experiences, and watch their children develop unexpected skills and confidence.

She has traveled on her own dime to learn new teaching techniques that she can pass on to the staff and parents. In 2014, she got an increasingly rare U.S. grant to visit Nevada to see how schools there help educate kids like hers to be responsible and potentially join the workforce. While Russian employers might sometimes take on a challenged individual, Elena says they do it only because "it's a nice thing to do. They expect and demand nothing." She adds, "This only reinforces a sense of inadequacy. In America, I saw that such young people can do something real with a sense of reward, even if it's only stuffing shopping bags or sweeping the floor."

When officials saw what Elena had pulled off, they were quick to claim credit and eager to be photographed at the center. Yet the truth is, the local government has provided almost no assistance.

At times, when donations flagged, Elena has had to delay salaries, but using her powers of persuasion and her connections, she's at least resolved that problem. She finally wangled a way to get her teachers on the books of local schools.

In its first year, the center was able to help 183 families, a tiny fraction of those needing assistance. Starry Rain now advises 700 families, with others hoping to spin off their own centers in distant towns. Elena holds constant fund-raisers copied from abroad; there are theatrical performances featuring the kids, sports competitions, and bake sales. The first group of parents, who helped build the center, were totally engaged. Those who have since benefited from the center's achievements don't always understand what it takes to keep all this going. They assume the government is behind it. That's what people here are used to, and Elena says she has to do more to make parents understand they are the foundation. It's all part of a changing Russia. She's started a fee-paying school for kids with less serious learning problems. Her hope is that the two centers will support each other.

The backing of a local well-known TV journalist has been a great help. Margarita Pavlova's younger daughter was diagnosed with severe autism. Though advised to give her up to state care, Pavlova, like Elena, refused. But everyone she turned to was utterly ignorant about how to proceed. As late as 2010, Pavlova says autism was not publicly discussed or seriously studied, and despite her best efforts she says progress remains painfully slow: "Specialists here have been useless, relying on decades-old information while the rest of the world has moved forward trying new methods and new research with some positive results." Her child now attends Starry Rain.

Pavlova left her job as a journalist to become the regional ombudsman for family and child issues. She says she realized one key thing: "How I look at my child, with love and determination, affects how society sees her and others like her."

One of Pavlova's first endeavors has been to draft a new code of ethics so that doctors can never again do what they tried to do to her and others—scare and pressure them into giving up a child. She has also launched a public campaign to educate the public about children like hers and demand the government fulfill its public promises of rehabilitation, education, and quality medical care.

Elena recalls a recent "historic" event. She got a letter from the city social work department asking for her help in persuading parents not to give up their children with Down's. "They asked us for help!" she exclaims.

Another big change afoot is the slow but evolving acceptance of adoption and foster care. Traditionally, Russians only adopted a child if they could pass off the newborn as their own. A woman would often pretend to be pregnant in order to mask an adoption. And as it was in the West for so many years, adopted children were rarely told about their start in life. In Russia, this meant that any infant too old "to pass" was doomed to a state orphanage.

During the financial troubles of the late 1980s and the 1990s, Russian orphanages saw their funding cut while the number of children left at their doors grew. Some of those children were so-called social orphans, abandoned by parents who could not afford to care for them or placed in state care because their parents had lost their parental rights due to drug addiction, alcoholism, or a prison sentence. The system was overwhelmed, and a desperate Russia allowed foreign adoptions for the first time.

After 1990, Americans adopted more than sixty thousand Russian children, but as Russia began to recover, there were growing calls "to stop exporting our children." More and more Russians considered foreign adoption a national embarrassment and shame. In 2005, Nadezhda Gartman, then head of child welfare in Chelyabinsk, came out against foreign adoption except in extreme cases. Nearing tears, she told me, "I was on a plane to Moscow. A foreign couple had just adopted a child. I had the feeling they were taking away my child, and I told my staff we will only give them up after we have done everything possible to find Russian parents for them or if their medical problems are such we cannot properly care for them here."

Over the years, rules and regulations were tightened to give Russians a first crack at the youngest, healthiest children available. While Russian authorities gradually made it easier for domestic adoptions, there weren't many takers. Meanwhile, it took longer and longer and became more and more expensive for foreigners to adopt—even though this left Russian children in orphanages during their first critical years, compounding any physical and psychological problems.

Opposition to foreign adoption continued to brew. The Russian media made headlines with highly emotional stories of foreign adoptions gone horribly wrong, highlighting the deaths of nineteen Russian children in the care of American families. Two cases got particular coverage, heavily influencing public opinion. In 2008, twenty-one-month-old Dmitry Yakovlev died of heatstroke after his American adoptive father left him in a hot car for nine hours. When his father was later acquitted of involuntary manslaughter by a Virginia court, there was widespread outrage at the country's leniency. In 2010, a seven-year-old boy was sent alone on a flight back to Russia by his adoptive mother in Tennessee. She included a typewritten note saying the boy had developmental and extreme behavioral problems she could no longer handle.

In response, Russian authorities suspended U.S. adoptions until the two countries could reach an agreement on greater screening for prospective parents. But when the long-fought-for agreement was finally signed, U.S.-Russian relations were breaking down again. The U.S. Congress passed the Magnitsky law, which imposed sanctions on Russian officials in response to the death in prison of Sergei Magnitsky, a thirty-seven-year-old Russian lawyer who had tried to expose a huge government tax

fraud at the expense of an American investment fund. His supporters say Magnitsky was deliberately denied proper medical
care and ultimately beaten to death. Russian authorities called
the Magnitsky law an arrogant insult and unjustified interference
in Russia's domestic politics. Russia's parliament retaliated by
banning American adoptions.

Moscow's opposition movement, then in its heyday, held an
emotional march against the adoption ban. Their slogan was
"Protect our orphans from mean officials." Their protests, highlighting the state's inability to care for the country's orphans, were
not replicated elsewhere in the country. Russians largely bought
into the often hysterical state-run media reports putting American adoptive parents in the worst possible light. Elected officials
declared a self-sufficient country should take care of its own.

In Chelyabinsk, social workers were quietly appalled by the
adoption ban. They knew that the government was still incapable
of adequately caring for the large number of Russian orphans.
They knew that efforts to increase domestic adoption and fostering were not making a dent. Every day, a popular local Web site
features a child eligible for adoption with an endearing photograph, a few lines about his or her adoption, and the words "I
want a mother." But of five thousand children in Chelyabinsk orphanages, only two hundred were adopted by Russians in 2012.
The numbers haven't increased much since then. And despite all
the publicity about the American mother who returned a difficult
child, officials admit the same thing happens in Russia not infre-
quently, though it is not publicly reported.

Irina Butorina is a young official with the region's social services department. She is blunt, extremely competent, and hard-
working. "If in the past only parents who couldn't have children
considered adoption, we now see Russians who may already have
kids approaching us because they think it is the right thing to
do." But she says the pool of families willing and able to adopt is

still small, and unlike foreigners, especially Americans, they are usually unwilling to adopt children with disabilities.

As the foreign adoption debate intensified, a fourteen-year-old Chelyabinsk orphan was snagged in the political net. Maxim Kargopoltsev had been in constant contact for several years with an American couple, Mil and Dianna Wallen, of Woodstock, Virginia. They first met Maxim while doing volunteer work through their church at his orphanage. Maxim had developmental problems, and in 2011 the Wallens decided to adopt him, worried what would become of him if he was left in state care. In anticipation of moving to America, Maxim added the Wallen name to his on his Facebook page. But his adoption was stopped because of the Magnitsky law. When his case was publicized, Sergei Vainshtein, a Chelyabinsk member of parliament and rabid nationalist, told Russian TV viewers it was important for Russian families to adopt more children. He said he was prepared to take Maxim under his guardianship. He bought the boy a cell phone and paid for him to have a holiday, but that turned out to be the extent of his "guardianship." Maxim was never absorbed into his family and remained in the orphanage. The Wallens have stayed in touch, Skyping regularly. After watching their press campaign fail, Maxim and the Wallens are now afraid to talk to reporters lest it only make matters worse.

Russian orphanages are not, overall, as bad as most Americans have been led to believe, but they are state institutions and vary greatly depending on who's in charge. It's impossible to fault the conditions at Chelyabinsk Orphanage No. 8, a well-maintained facility with caring staff. The director, Tatiana Smirnova, reorganized the place so that children are split up into groups of ten, which she calls "families." The family units are cozy, with caregivers ready to help with homework and other issues, though Smirnova struggles to find adequate psychological expertise. She has no illusions her orphanage, however much improved, is any replacement for a real family with real parents. She would prefer those parents be Russians, but when I last spoke to her, she believed foreign adoption was still necessary.

Her biggest challenge, and one much discussed by others in Russian social services, is preparing these children for the real world. Smirnova says it may sound strange, but children coming out of Russia's orphanages are much less independent, and much less prepared to take care of themselves, than children brought up in a normal family setting. Concerned about perceptions of child labor, the orphanages no longer have the youngsters in their care do laundry or cooking. They are not asked to dig vegetables in the orphanage garden. They have no idea how to handle money. They end up with none of the skills they need to live on their own when the time comes. They are used to receiving handouts, because providing orphans with cell phones and clothing supplies has become fashionable. Those handouts disappear when kids leave orphanages at eighteen. Smirnova encourages well-wishers to do more than give presents or host yet another feel-good Christmas party. She says these kids desperately need mentors, visits to prospective job sites, and weekends with real families, to get a taste for real family life and responsibilities.

Asked about the fate of those who leave the orphanages at eighteen, Irina Butorina, with social services, calls this a "touchy, difficult subject." Her studies show that at most only 30 percent can anticipate a modest, stable family life, with the rest ending up in prison or somehow falling through the cracks. Orphans allegedly receive state housing when they go out on their own, but it is often little better than a rat-infested single room. If they do end up in a desirable space, these inexperienced kids are preyed on by scam artists who persuade them to sign over the property for a small amount of cash. Worse still, some orphanage staff take advantage of these kids, appropriating their apartments. In theory, it's a good program. In practice, there are problems.

The ban on U.S. adoptions has been expanded to include

any country that permits gay marriage. That has severely limited
foreign adoptions. NGOs and Chelyabinsk social workers anticipate thousands of orphans will remain locked in institutions for
the foreseeable future.

Those most at risk are the physically and mentally challenged,
for whom conditions remain poor. When twenty-three-year-old
Nastya Platonova, a Chelyabinsk resident, tried to foster a child
with a rare genetic disease, she met obstacles at every turn and
could only conclude the Moscow orphanage where the child was
housed did not want to lose the two-thousand-dollar-a-month
subsidy it received.

Masha, as she has since come to be called, had been abandoned at birth and diagnosed with Treacher Collins syndrome,
a rare condition characterized by absent cheekbones, malformed
or absent ears, hearing loss, and downward-slanting eyes. Masha
was consigned to a Moscow orphanage for special-needs children,
where she did not get special, let alone basic, care, despite more than
enough government support.

When Nastya first saw three-year-old Masha, she was malnourished and terrified of everything and everyone. She was unable to talk or walk. She had been supplied with hearing aids, but
the staff had never taken them out of the box. There was panic
in the orphanage when Nastya brought Masha new clothes. The
reason became clear as Nastya undressed her. Masha was covered
in bruises, evidently from being beaten. Nastya videotaped the
conditions, though on the advice of the NGO helping her, she
never went public. She was warned officials might retaliate by
refusing to let her take Masha.

As it was, the orphanage staff told Nastya she was crazy for
wanting such a child, dismissing Masha as a vegetable who would
never develop. They did everything possible to stop Nastya from
taking her. The head of the orphanage said Masha's birth mother
wanted to retrieve her. It wasn't true. Nastya, who had been approved as a foster mother, surmised the staff was loath to let her

go because this disabled child was worth money. Other foster parents I spoke to raised similar concerns. In this case, the authorities seriously underestimated Nastya. She ultimately went before a commission of twenty people to present her case. She left the room and went outside in the cold to wait, convinced she had failed. A man rushed up, late for the commission meeting. They spoke, and he cast the deciding ballot in her favor.

When I first met her in 2012, Nastya could have been mistaken for a beguiling teenager. In her mid-twenties, she was slim, with long blond hair, dressed in jeans and a T-shirt. She already had a healthy son of her own, but she believed God told her to foster or adopt another child. Initially, she had planned on taking in a healthy little girl, but as she flipped through data banks on the Internet, she came across Masha in the files of a Russian NGO that promotes adoption and fostering. She said, "I immediately knew she was mine." Despite her facial deformities, there is indeed something about Masha that reminds you of Nastya. Her husband initially went along with the plan, but their respective parents were appalled at the idea of a "deformed" grandchild. Her husband got cold feet, and when he backed out, their marriage dissolved. Nastya went ahead, refiling all the burdensome paperwork, this time as a single mother.

She chose to foster rather than adopt because adoptive parents get no financial benefits, while fostering provides subsidies— although at four hundred dollars a month for a challenged child it is a far cry from what the orphanage was getting. Her relatives have been less than supportive. People on the streets have shunned her, put off by Masha's appearance. Some have snidely suggested she took Masha only for the money, though subsidies and so-called free medicine have covered only a fraction of the subsequent operations and psychological therapy Masha has needed. Nastya has paid what she can, and the Moscow NGO, which helped her find Masha in the first place, has provided the balance for expensive medical care and counseling. Nastya is also a regular at Elena Zhernova's Starry Rain center, where she says sensory training, gymnastic classes, speech therapy, and a community of like parents have made all the difference. She's found an unusually talented psychologist in another city. It's a three-hour bus ride there and back.

After becoming a member of Nastya's family, Masha, now a gangly eight-year-old, can hear. She can talk. She can run. After what seemed an interminable period when she clung to Nastya, she now laughs, plays with her brother and others, and grows ever more confident. Given how mysterious her rare condition is, she is developing far faster than anyone anticipated. It's been a struggle, marked by severe emotional outbursts and frightening tantrums, but with each month Masha makes progress. There have been moments when Nastya says she didn't think she could handle the challenges, but as Masha curls up next to her, Nastya says it's not just Masha who has changed dramatically. She has too. "She has been a gift. I have learned so much about values, and self-knowledge, everything because of her."

EIGHT

THE DOCTORS

In the turbulent 1990s, Dr. Eduard Reebin was the head of Chelyabinsk City Hospital No. 8 and happy to welcome me. Hastily built in the 1930s to accommodate the influx of workers sent to man Stalin's frantic industrial development, No. 8 remained a sprawling, haphazard jigsaw of two- and three-story buildings with nothing but muddy or icy pathways to link them. Getting from one medical department to another, doctors, nurses, and patients trudged through snow in winter, sludge in spring. It was hardly efficient and definitely not sanitary. There were no elevators, and the cement stairways were so irregularly worn down and slippery as to be death defying.

Catering to the Tractor Factory region of the city, Hospital No. 8 was overcrowded with twice as many patients as originally planned. There were no specialized hospital beds, let alone emergency call buttons. Forget about individual patient monitors. Equipment was primitive. Dr. Reebin looked at me with raised eyebrows when I asked about such things as adequate dialysis machines or respirators, especially those designed for children. He was struggling just to get basic antibiotics and anesthesia.

Health care in the Soviet Union had always promised far more than it could deliver. Though the care was technically free, patients often had to bring their own sheets and pillows, not to mention gloves for operations and most medicines. Diagnosis was more miss than hit. If a patient wanted less than a massive scar, he or she had to provide the surgical thread. There were some world-class specialists to be found in the Kremlin Clinic or other hospitals usually catering to the Communist Party elite, but the average doctor was no more than what we consider a physician's assistant. When the Soviet Union was falling apart, the situation initially only got worse, but the door had finally opened to the rest of the world.

That door cracked open in Chelyabinsk in the early hours of June 4, 1989, when word spread of a terrible accident involving children, the sort of thing that galvanizes attention. Sparks from two passing trains, packed with kids going to summer camp, ignited a low-lying cloud of industrial gas that was hugging the tracks. There were explosions and hundreds of casualties. Hospitals were flooded with young burn victims. Soviet doctors had neither the means nor the training to treat the victims. In an unusual move, Soviet officials hid neither the accident nor the resulting problems. Western colleagues immediately volunteered their services and were allowed in, even to the military-industrial hub of Chelyabinsk, which was still closed to all foreigners.

The Western staff, including doctors and nurses, brought welcome medicines and expertise. They suggested new ways to think about infection control, saving many lives. Some were as simple as using liquid soap instead of germ-infested bars lying in fetid water. They taught their Soviet counterparts new surgical techniques. They brought in and introduced pressure bandages, a relatively simple way to limit scarring and crippling deformation. This early collaboration was the beginning of further exchanges.

A burly man in his mid-forties, Dr. Reebin at Hospital No. 8 was excited at the idea of cooperation. When I first spoke to him in 1993, dozens of disposable gloves, washed for reuse, were laid out to dry. He was frantically scrambling to find X-ray film. He was dependent on inconsistent Western aid for fundamentals like antibiotics. But in the midst of shock and chaos, he hoped, at last, to expand direct contact with Western doctors to learn from them and improve care. He hoped that the Internet, just reaching Chelyabinsk, would be a great teaching tool. And with new opportunities to travel to the West, he hoped to avoid the corrupt middlemen in the Ministry of Health to purchase better and cheaper equipment by himself.

He did the research, and he saw that he could get a lot better for less on his own. We met again by chance on his return flight from the United States. Coiled around his neck, like a bizarre snake, was what can only be described as a very strange piece of jewelry. It was a secondhand endoscope, for him a precious and rare piece of fiber-optic equipment that would allow him to improve the diagnosis of gastrointestinal problems. American doctors had given it to him, and lest it be stolen en route, he wore it close to his heart the entire journey.

But once he got back to the hospital, his momentary euphoria was short-lived. It was 1995. The economic situation in Chelyabinsk had deteriorated even more in his short absence. His already inadequate budget was slashed by 50 percent. So much for new equipment, let alone salaries and medicines.

He started to barter. There was a company that couldn't pay its taxes and was threatened with fines or worse. "I did a deal with the director," he explained. "'You are in debt for such and such amount. Our hospital will take your products for that amount; that will go against your taxes.'"

Reebin ended up with pipes and, amazingly, found buyers the company couldn't. He traded them for fish and meat products. He then brought the food supplies back to Chelyabinsk, sold them on the market, and with that money paid for salaries and medicines.

Because of his manipulations to save the hospital, he was accused of corruption. He would spend nights poring over documents to make sure everything was accounted for. He says the bottom line was that local officials wanted to shake him down for a part of the money he had made for the hospital. He refused, and somehow survived.

Not only that. He was subsequently elected from his neighborhood to serve on the city council. He was initially encouraged by the stability that emerged when Vladimir Putin succeeded Boris Yeltsin as president. Reebin tried to improve the region's health care, lobbied hard for money and got it, but then watched as it was eaten up by poor management, cronyism, lack of strategic thinking, and ever-growing corruption.

When we last met, the now-retired Reebin was in despair. He said corruption was only getting worse. I asked if he had been encouraged by the much-publicized arrest of the Chelyabinsk region's minister of health and several colleagues. They were swept up in a dramatic, videotaped raid while they sat in a sauna dividing up millions of dollars in ill-gotten gains. They had put in exorbitant receipts for cheap, substandard equipment, pocketing the difference, the common corruption technique. Their arrest had sent shock waves through the city, but Reebin was not impressed. He suggested the arrests were not part of a real crackdown; it was just that the minister, long fingered for corruption, had simply not paid up the chain. He believes tenders for medical equipment are regularly rigged.

One of his daughters joined us at a central café, near the city parade ground, still graced by a towering statue of Lenin. Spurred by her and a shot of single malt, Reebin talked about his past for the first time. His grandparents grew up in a village where they had enough land to feed their family. By the late 1920s and into the 1930s, such people were condemned as "kulaks," so-called rich peasants. They were arrested, and their meager property and belongings confiscated.

His mother, still only in her early teens, went to live with an older brother in Chelyabinsk, where she worked in one of the new industrial plants. One day she was fifteen minutes late to work. She was sentenced to prison, but the Germans suddenly invaded, war broke out, and instead she was sent as a "volunteer" to the front. There she met Roman, an Armenian from the Soviet republic of Georgia. They fell in love. She became pregnant and was evacuated home. They promised to marry after the war. Roman never appeared.

Reebin says he grew up knowing nothing about his father. His mother merely said he had been killed in the war. Reebin conjured up images of his father as a hero, a valiant secret agent who died defending his country. But on holidays, no one acknowledged his father. The family received no special holiday food packages, like those for other veterans. He finally figured out something was wrong and pressed his mother. She confessed his father had abandoned them.

Reebin studied to be a pilot, and while he was at an aviation institute, he met someone from Georgia. "We talked, and I told him my father was from Georgia. He helped me locate him, and we decided I should go there and confront the son of a bitch."

He did. When he rang the bell of the apartment, an old woman answered the door. She gasped when she saw Reebin. It seems he could have been his father's twin. She told him where he could find Roman at work. "I was ready for justice," says Reebin. When he met his father, the reaction was not what he expected. His father looked at him with a mixture of shock, astonishment, and joy. Reebin remembers him sputtering again and again, with a question in his voice, "Edik, Edik?" That was the name the young parents-to-be had agreed to call their baby were he a boy. When Reebin then confronted his father with accusations he had abandoned both him and his mother, his father had another story to tell. He showed Reebin the letter he had received from the Urals telling him his wife and son had both perished in childbirth. "To have a father after all those years,"

Reebin said, sighing. Roman subsequently urged him to leave the air force and become a doctor.

It was a profession Reebin adored. He married a doctor, and Reebin then encouraged (they would say forced) his two daughters to become doctors. They have since quit because of intolerable conditions and salaries. Reebin now finds himself trying to dissuade his beloved granddaughter from following in the family tradition. "It's a mess," he says.

Since I first met Reebin more than two decades ago, health care in Russia has improved dramatically, but it is indeed a mess: an incomprehensible mix of free care, as promised by the government, under-the-table payments, quotas, and corruption. The result is a capricious combination of excellent and substandard care. There are now new regional cardiology and cancer centers in Chelyabinsk but only one surgeon qualified to operate on children. There is plenty of pseudoscience left over from the Soviet period, when medical practice advocated radon baths and ultraviolet light machines, cheap treatments the rest of the world has long dismissed as ineffective or outright dangerous.

Doctors complain that medical education is worse, not better, with students able to buy their way in and out of medical school because professors do not receive adequate salaries for their work. And because medical salaries are ridiculously low—a few hundred dollars a month—only three out of a class of twenty might stay in the profession, with the rest using their training to seek better-paying jobs in the pharmaceutical industry or related medical businesses. Those who stay seek out specialties, like plastic surgery, where they can make extra money.

Igor Skripkov, a dedicated intensive care doctor, is hard-pressed to find students willing to join his specialty because it's one of the least lucrative. He is excited that the Internet and Skype allow him to consult with colleagues around the world on tough cases, but he faces a shortage of skilled doctors in his department.

He is frustrated by poor pay, a continued lack of equipment such as individual patient monitors, and a city hospital that should basically be torn down. Though only twenty years old, his hospital, like Reebin's No. 8, is a haphazard collection of buildings, with leaking roofs and peeling walls. The director, by all accounts an honest man, is doing his best, but he doesn't have much to work with. Asked how he managed, Skripkov, now in his fifties, replied, "We have brains and golden hands. My generation at least is used to creating something out of nothing."

In cities, medical service is much better than in outlying communities, where living conditions are unattractive. The government promised general practitioners huge benefits if they would go to the countryside, but then failed to follow up. In the city of Chelyabinsk, a doctor will still make a house call to attend to a sick child, demonstrating the best of what socialized medicine can provide. In more remote villages, you can wait forever for an ambulance to arrive in the event of a life-threatening emergency such as a heart attack. Elderly patients I have spoken to in villages say doctors reject them, saying, "You are old, what else do you want?" Yet I also know eighty-year-olds in the city who have received excellent free treatment, with a paid stay in a state-subsidized sanatorium for recuperation.

One friend in Chelyabinsk city is embarrassed that she pays bribes, but she says she has no choice. "If my grandson is sick, I have to offer money, or the doctor will not look after him as he should. I know that I shouldn't do this, because I am only perpetuating corruption and nothing will change, but what can I do when it's my grandson's health? I choose my grandson."

Access to specialists and good care is a constant source of discussion and ultimately depends on luck, contacts, or money. Medication is also a conundrum. The government provides only certain medicines for free. Those on the government list are often neither the best nor the most effective. A doctor will prescribe what is free but then advise patients to purchase more appropriate medications, usually foreign, at a private pharmacy for substantial sums of money that many can't afford. Alarmed by the country's dependence on foreign-made medicines, nationalists in parliament have broached cutting imports. That idea was met with protests across the Internet, but President Dmitry Medvedev nonetheless said 90 percent of medicines must come from domestic stocks by 2018. That's a tall order.

The heavy reliance on both foreign medicines and foreign medical equipment is putting the Russian health-care system in a bind, with costs rising fast due to the ruble's dramatic fall against the dollar. While a decision on medicines has been put off, efforts are already under way to cut back on the import of foreign devices. Applications by foreign companies to take part in state tenders will be denied if there are two or more entries from Russia or fellow Eurasian Economic Union members like Belarus, Armenia, and Kazakhstan, none known for their expertise in the medical field. Given that just 5 percent of surgical equipment is currently supplied by Russian firms, doctors like Skripkov, who already face inadequate equipment, anticipate the problem getting even worse. He says even his creativity may not be enough to compensate for the changes.

To supplement doctors' base salaries, hospitals are now permitted to treat up to 15 percent of their patient load for a fee. These patients get attentive care in more comfortable surroundings. In fact, most every hospital administrator far exceeds the legal limits for paid services, often leaving "free" patients in long lines or hallways.

And to cater to a growing demand for good and timely care, private clinics are now allowed to treat certain conditions. Just walk down the streets of downtown Chelyabinsk and you will see shingles advertising private dental care, most of which is not covered by the state, ophthalmic services, allergy treatment, family medicine, and fertility clinics as well as plastic surgery. Given their expertise (I have seen their excellent work) and their low prices,

Russian plastic surgeons now attract many European customers. A thirty-thousand-dollar face-lift in the West is perhaps two thousand dollars in Russia in a modern, clean clinic. This is steep for most locals but not for foreigners. But plastic surgeons who specialize in burns, not the reduction of buttocks, recently went on strike to protest cutbacks and lack of support.

From 150 private clinics in 2003, there are now more than 700 in Chelyabinsk city alone. A doctor working just one day a week at a private clinic can make more than his monthly state salary. According to Dr. Tatiana Pestova, the government is gradually shrinking state facilities for certain specialties and depending on private doctors like her more and more, though it does not admit this publicly.

Dr. Pestova is the head doctor in a private gynecological and fertility clinic that has made up for the shortcomings of the government system. Despite the Kremlin's concern about an anemic birthrate, state fertility services are hard to access. Until 2009, couples in Chelyabinsk had to travel hundreds if not thousands of miles to find state services, where they then waited in long lines. Since then, one government-sponsored fertility clinic has opened here, but it caters to only 150 couples a year, a tiny fraction of demand. Couples hoping to get in on the program must be vetted and approved by a government commission, by all accounts subject to corruption. Women over the age of forty are not eligible, and medicines for in vitro, which typically cost twenty-five hundred dollars, are not included.

Dr. Pestova, who trained in England, has five thousand patients a year. IVF treatment is ten thousand dollars. Her office is spotless and welcoming, with a rare air of efficiency. There are no long lines. Pestova says she demands a huge amount from her doctors and pays them accordingly—ten times what they would make at a city hospital. She claims her success rate is comparable to any in the West. She has also developed an egg and sperm donor program, which the state does not yet offer in Chelya-binsk.

The profession that Dr. Eduard Reebin so loved, and for which he once had great hope, does not get high ratings from Russians today—with less than a third saying they are satisfied. After more than two decades of discussing the subject, Reebin says, "Free quality health care under current conditions is a myth—rubbish, absolute rubbish."

NINE

THE ADDICTS

One night in 2010, a gray van pulls off to the side of the road and parks. Every evening it idles in one of the Chelyabinsk neighborhoods where Soviet-style apartment blocks, much like the worst of American public housing, predominate. The van waits for someone to knock on the door. There's nothing to indicate where it's from or what it's for. Its schedule isn't publicized, but those who need to know find out.

The team wedged inside includes a doctor, a psychologist, and a former drug addict who all work for Compass, the region's sole government-supported AIDS and drug outreach center. Compass, inspired by Western experience, was founded in the 1990s when U.S. and European funding was readily available and officially welcomed. It now receives modest support from the local budget.

Russian officials were slow to address the issues of drug use and HIV. Experts here now estimate at least one in every hundred Chelyabinsk residents is infected. This is more than twice the Russian national average, which in turn is now twice that of the United States. And HIV infection rates continue to grow, with the Urals and Siberia at the top of the list.

The explosion of HIV was triggered by the sharp rise in heroin use in the post-Soviet 1990s. Chelyabinsk was hit particularly hard because it is a major transit point for drugs traveling north from Afghanistan, where Russian officials complain the U.S. military did little to stop poppy production. Some go so far as to say the United States has deliberately tried to get Russians hooked.

Back in the Compass van, twenty-seven-year-old Dr. Natalia Golubiya projects a different image from the staff at state-run clinics, where expertise in drug addiction and HIV treatment remains inadequate and censorious. In tight jeans and a red sweater, she lays out patient files, latex gloves, needles, and test tubes on a narrow table. No one talks much. It's warm inside, but bitter on the dark streets. Wind whips snow into swirls. The team isn't sure anyone will venture out. Then there's a knock, and the van door slides open. A young woman climbs in, dripping sleet, followed by her five-year-old child. The woman has come to get her test results. Golubiya immediately recognizes them and breaks into a smile. She has good news. The woman, a heroin addict, is HIV negative. On hearing this, she barely responds and is about to leave when Golubiya says there's more. Like almost all who come in for testing, the woman is positive for hepatitis C. Golubiya gives her advice on what to do next and provides a supply of clean needles.

Golubiya and her team do not suggest methadone, an internationally accepted treatment for heroin addiction. That's because it is banned in Russia, denounced by officials as just another form of poison. Instead, the official policy is to encourage immediate abstinence, rather than the gradual progress methadone-substitution therapy entails. Many experts in drug treatment condemn this approach as ineffective, saying that addiction is a much more complex and intractable challenge and that a quick detox cannot, in most cases, bring a lasting cure. Yet just discussing methadone's pros and cons can provoke violent protests, even legal action. In Moscow, a Kremlin-based youth group broke up a symposium where scientists were looking into its possible benefits. They denounced the organizers as criminals and paid agents of the West. Officials have also threatened scientists who posted information about methadone research on their Web sites.

With so much on her plate, Dr. Golubiya just shrugs when asked about the methadone debate, or the lack thereof. She is grateful Compass has at least managed to get permission for a needle-exchange program. It may not end addiction, but having seen the results of needle exchanges in the West, she believes they are one way to help limit the spread of HIV. Yet needle programs too are controversial (as they are in the United States). Golubiya says many are against them, hence the anonymity of the van. Compass wants to avoid problems. "Many think drug addicts and those infected with HIV should be isolated," she says when the woman and child have disappeared into the night. "Despite ongoing information campaigns," she explains, "many still don't know enough, and many just don't want to know."

■

Compass continues its regular forays through the city to test and treat those at risk. It has expanded its education programs. But the needle-exchange program has been dropped, and the staff, which once welcomed foreign funders and reporters with open arms, is now no longer willing to meet. Sergei Avdeev, a young doctor who started and still oversees the Compass program, has embarked on a promising political career, which requires unquestioning adherence to Putin's policies. Once upon a time, we talked openly about the region's problems, the pernicious effect of widespread homophobia on HIV treatment, and his regret at the government's attacks on foreign funding and joint ventures. Such discussions are clearly no longer going to advance his aspirations.

One key figure, however, defies official warnings against interviews. Dr. Alexander Viguzov, who has spearheaded the fight in Chelyabinsk against HIV and AIDS, is chief of the region's Infectious Disease Center. It's been an uphill battle. He picks up a letter he recently received from the local Ministry of Social

Welfare. It asks whether an infected child can live in an orphanage. "They still think HIV is caught like a cold and don't realize there are already dozens of HIV kids in the region's orphanages." For a moment, this usually contained man loses it, furious with continued ignorance. "Even though we keep working with them, they keep asking the same damned questions."

Viguzov identified the first AIDS case in Chelyabinsk back in 1990. The first patient was gay. Given extremely negative attitudes toward homosexuality and an economic and political crisis, local authorities decided the disease wasn't much of a problem, and certainly wasn't a priority. Dr. Viguzov thought otherwise. He saw the data coming out of Moscow, where the first Russian AIDS case was discovered in 1986. He got information from abroad. He understood the growing danger. Despite his warnings, local officials ignored him for more than six years. In the meantime, drug use exploded, and HIV spread rapidly, with no efforts to prevent it. Viguzov believes local officials only began to pay attention when the issue hit home—when their own children started using intravenous drugs and got infected.

Thanks to Viguzov, access to medicine for those infected is not a problem here. He says he has the equivalent of whatever pills are available in the West—though he now worries that with rising budget deficits the Ministry of Health will start buying cheap copies in India and China, which are not as effective. The biggest problem he faces is that so many of the infected do not come to him, and many who do come too late. It's the same issue American doctors confront but with added complications.

U.S. physicians also battle the stigma of HIV. And in America, too, the perception that you must have done something "wrong" to get infected leads many to resist testing. But this problem is particularly strong in Russia, where treatment in outlying regions is often inadequate as well as censorious and assurances of anonymity are regularly violated.

Renad, a skinny young man in a black baseball cap, catches

sight of Viguzov in the center's hallway and dashes up to give him a hug. Viguzov beams. Renad is one of his success stories. "He knows his blood counts. I love it when I can talk to a patient about details. When he understands his levels, it means he is involved in his treatment."

Renad has to travel several hours to reach the center and the assurance of confidentiality. A former addict, he can't reveal he has AIDS in his village, or he would be ostracized and lose his job as a mechanic. "This isn't the West," he explains. "By law, they can't fire me, but the law doesn't matter. If I told anyone, there would be real problems, and it's not going to change anytime soon."

Viguzov has tried to transform the once-forbidding regional Infectious Disease Center into a welcoming place for all who need help. But as the numbers have grown, the space has become far from adequate, and he is understaffed. He struggles to find doctors willing to go into the field. As is so often the case in the medical profession, the pay is ridiculously low, a few hundred dollars a month, and there is no opportunity to make more on the side, as there is for other specialists who can work in their free time at private clinics. In the five years I've known him, he's always been passionate and determined. Now in his mid-sixties, with a shock of white hair, Viguzov shows the first signs of despair.

It looked as if he were making progress—the numbers of newly infected had stabilized by 2009—but in 2012 the numbers jumped from two thousand new cases a year to three thousand. They jumped again in 2013. Sharing needles remains the primary cause, but a growing number of new cases are women, infected through unprotected sex and identified only when they are already pregnant. A large number of them also seem to be drug users who were infected years ago but who put off testing and treatment until their symptoms exploded. Viguzov can't begin to estimate how many infected people are still out there, refusing to be tested, despite treatment that will save their lives, all the while infecting others.

With unprotected sexual activity and drug use as common as anywhere in the West, Russians are still playing catch-up. When I first spoke to him in 2010, Dr. Viguzov said there was no effective program to engage educators and doctors, who were still embarrassed to discuss sex and the transmission of HIV. It hasn't helped that the head of Russia's Youth Services condemns sex education in schools, declaring in only the vaguest terms that nineteenth-century Russian literature and the Orthodox Church are the best teachers.

Viguzov has his hands full trying to battle what he calls "Neanderthals." His organization, woefully understaffed, has little support to provide counseling and spread the word. He is constantly on the road, with the passion of a missionary, training teachers, student leaders, union representatives, and psychologists. Once concentrated in the city of Chelyabinsk, drug use and HIV are now spiking in outlying villages and desolate mining towns, where rates of one in one hundred are not uncommon. During a trip to a distant village where several people had been diagnosed with HIV, he said he confronted the "old thinking" that HIV somehow isn't Russian, that "normal" people will not be affected. He says women who refuse to continue being tested after mandatory prenatal checks are getting infected and then passing on the virus to healthy newborns through their breast milk. He regularly meets with local Muslim leaders and Orthodox priests, who have been slow to get involved, convinced that AIDS is a curse from God. He hopes he has persuaded some to take a more generous, compassionate, and educated approach.

In the Soviet Union, condoms were crude and seldom used. A wide selection of Western brands is now available at every supermarket checkout. Russian versions of magazines like *Cosmopolitan* have increasingly taken on the issue of safe sex, but Viguzov says risky behavior remains a huge problem. Too often, women are loath to demand their partners wear condoms for fear it will be a turnoff. "I am afraid of being infected," they tell him, "but I am even more afraid of being left alone." He tries to get community leaders to talk about not just sex but the nature of relationships. When I ask him what is happening with the gay community, given legal restrictions on open discussions, he just shakes his head, saying, "It's anyone's guess."

Viguzov sees the biggest problem of all as easy access to drugs. He cites the rise of drug use and HIV in Ozersk, a "closed" nuclear weapons city with 100,000 residents. Given that Ozersk is accessible only via one road where all cars and people are checked and the internal security is extremely tight, he suggests federal agents have to be in on the narcotics trade.

Viguzov is also depressed by the lack of adequate treatment for addicts. President Putin has said courts may now mandate treatment for addicts who come before them, but there are few state rehab clinics, and experts widely condemn the treatment they provide as crude, brutal, and ineffective. Dr. Maria Kolosova says addicts are rendered comatose for the first two weeks, pumped full of sedatives to keep them quiet while they undergo detox, and then left with no follow-up therapy. The results, she says, are worse than useless. She is one of the many Viguzov sees abandoning the field. A young psychiatrist who worked with addicts, she has quit, not just because of the pathetic salary of two hundred dollars a month, but because she couldn't achieve anything given the primitive approach to care. She gets as much if not more money working as a hotel receptionist.

Rehab has largely been left to NGOs with no medical expertise and little or no oversight. One of the most controversial programs is called City Without Drugs. Its approach is harsh and coercive. Family members have paid employees of City Without Drugs to seize addicts and detain them in centers where they are then handcuffed to their beds and given a diet of water, bread, onions, and garlic during a detox period that takes weeks. It's then followed by months of forced imprisonment until "the addicts behave."

The center's organizers claim their "tough-it-out approach"

has a staggering 70 percent success rate, though the organization has actually never conducted a follow-up study. Its founder, Evgeny Roizman, is a handsome, charismatic personality who served a term in Russia's parliament. He has repeatedly said that HIV can be cured once an HIV-positive person stops using heroin, another claim that has no scientific backing. Yet given the epidemic of drug addiction and HIV and the few government programs, his center's harsh treatment has received support from the public as well as celebrities, the Orthodox Church, and even some human rights groups desperate for a solution.

Growing reports of kidnappings and forced detention, and the death of one young woman addict from apparent beatings, got some people rethinking his methods. Several of his staff members have been convicted for illegal activities, and the organization itself has openly admitted it has skirted the law. But City Without Drugs is still in operation, and in a major upset Roizman defeated the Kremlin's candidate in 2013 to become mayor of Yekaterinburg, the capital of the neighboring region of Sverdlovsk.

Dr. Viguzov is among those who applaud Roizman's efforts, as well as those of other NGOs. He believes they are much more successful than government programs. Still, most of the twenty or so independent rehab centers in Chelyabinsk remain voluntary and oppose Roizman's methods. Most are linked to Baptist and Pentecostal churches. Despite considerable suspicion of what many Russians pejoratively call "foreign sects," there is grudging respect for the churches' efforts on the addiction front.

The oldest rehab center in Chelyabinsk, linked to the New Life evangelical church, opened its doors in 2000. Up to a hundred or so addicts are housed in a run-down abandoned factory. They come, of their own free will, for a year's stay. Most pay about three hundred dollars a month, but for those who can't, the course of treatment is free. The conditions are spartan, with six or more residents sharing a small room. Men and women are separated; their only contact comes when the women supply meals they've cooked through a hatch and the men in turn push cleaned dishes back through the same hatch.

The program is based on abstinence, prayer, Bible study, and counseling by those who have already graduated. There is a strict daily schedule and punishments for infractions like swearing, smoking, or fighting. These include writing out biblical tracts a hundred or more times. The program director says 90 percent finish the year and then go on to a halfway house for another six months. It is a far longer program than anything offered by the government, with the promise of community support over the long term.

Anya Gartman is a high school dropout who injected heroin for ten years until she came to New Life at twenty-five. Her friends were dying. She was suicidal. The short government program, with no follow-up, had not worked. Then she met a young woman who told her about the program. Five years later, Anya is clean and employed at New Life. With clear blue eyes and long blond hair, simply dressed in a turtleneck and black jeans, she is an example for the desperate women she is now counseling. She says she was lucky because those currently coming to the center are often addicted to drugs far worse than heroin, which is being replaced by cheaper, more deadly concoctions. One drug that gained traction in 2013 was homemade "crocodile"; to make it, one mixes codeine, which was then widely sold over the counter, with gasoline, paint thinner, hydrochloric acid, iodine, and red phosphorus scraped from the striking pads on matchbooks.

"Crocodile" gets its name from the rotting it creates at the injection site. The addicts' skin becomes greenish and scalelike as blood vessels burst and the surrounding tissue dies. Eventually, users are covered in abscesses, their immune systems totally shot.

According to official statistics, more than seventy thousand Russians die each year of drug abuse, with the number of addicts skyrocketing. With roughly half the population of the United States, Russia now has about the same number of addicts.

TEN

SCHOOLHOUSES
AND BARRACKS

The most prestigious state secondary school in Chelyabinsk is Lyceum 31, which specializes in mathematics, physics, and IT. To enter, a student must attend Sunday classes, for a fee, for a year, to prove his or her skills and prepare for the rigorous program. Though a state school, it then charges parents the equivalent of an additional fifty dollars a month, a not insubstantial sum here. But it's an investment in their kids' future. These students often win national and international competitions, and most will get scholarships to the best universities in Moscow and St. Petersburg. Many then hope to go on to Harvard, MIT, Stanford, Oxford, or Cambridge. The country's best and brightest don't see their futures here, complaining, "There are not enough opportunities for informatics, math, physics, and economics." They say that Russia has yet to figure out that oil and gas are not as important as developing new talent and new industries.

These kids get their news from the Internet, with all but a few dismissing state-run TV as crude propaganda. Yet politics are hardly their main concern; they said not a word when their favorite news sites were either closed down or co-opted by the government. They are more concerned about acing their college entrance exams, and like high school kids everywhere they spend hours on the Internet chatting online via Facebook or its Russian equivalent, VKontakte, about relationships and the latest, coolest download. Their top sites include Google, Wikipedia, YouTube, and geeky blogs. Their musical preferences cover the range from classical to heavy metal; an assortment of Russian groups as well as Pink Floyd, AC/DC, and Deep Purple are among their current favorites. Their reading runs the gamut from Russian classics to fantasy of all types, including George Orwell's less-than-fantastical *1984*. They play the same online games as their peers in the West (*Defense of the Ancients* was popular when I visited) and download a wide range of Russian and Western movies, most of them pirated. They are fans of *Avatar*, *The Matrix*, *The Terminator*, *Life of Pi*, and *Game of Thrones* and look out for new flicks and TV shows. When asked who their heroes are, many said no one, with others listing a curious mix of Joseph Stalin, Steve Jobs, Bill Gates, and Gandhi. They cited not one current or past Russian opposition figure, not even Andrei Sakharov, one of the heroes of Russia's human rights movement.

I ask them about Vladimir Putin. This was before his popularity soared following the annexation of Crimea and intervention in eastern Ukraine. They supported him as the only possible president. Asked about the prospect of antigovernment demonstrations in Chelyabinsk, they all shook their heads. "Not going to happen," according to this chorus.

Russian schools struggle to keep good teachers, even the best ones like Lyceum 31. Starting salaries in 2013 had been raised, with much publicity, to the equivalent of $500 a month, but by 2014, with the ruble dropping in value, this pay and its buying power hovered at $250. Top salaries aren't dramatically better. Teachers have to find a second job or tutor many hours on the side to make a living wage.

Free and good education was once something Russians could be proud of, but secondary students may soon be limited to taking only four basic subjects without paying a fee for extras. Principals at allegedly free state schools with better reputations already demand "donations" to accept students, and parents are regularly pressured to subsidize the purchase of equipment and building improvements. In outlying benighted villages and small towns where parents can't pony up this kind of money and good teachers are hard to find, the conditions are now poor.

Irina Kunkildina and Tamara Khadusenko, both in their fifties, are devoted teachers who run a paid after-school program called Emergency Help associated with Lyceum 31. It's a way for the lyceum to provide opportunities for teachers to supplement their pay. It offers remedial classes, tutoring for university exams, and extras not available in state schools, like computer graphics.

Irina and Tamara have stayed in the profession, though there were times in the late 1980s and the 1990s when they didn't know how they would feed their families. Tamara recalls the panic when she could not breast-feed her daughter and there was no formula available. During summer vacations, Irina sold potatoes from the family plot. She was so ashamed that instead of marketing her produce in Chelyabinsk, she would travel two hours to Yekaterinburg so that her colleagues and students wouldn't see her. As you've heard, and will hear again, Irina and Tamara say it was women who saved their families because men were less ready to bury their pride and do whatever job it took to get by. They say they are among the lucky ones because their husbands don't drink and are finally making decent money, allowing them to do what they love most—teach. But they believe the legacy of the Soviet Union's demise has left men a lot weaker than women to this day. Like so many, they talk about the country's depleted gene pool: so many men were killed in the revolution, the civil war, the purges, and then World War II. They worry that the best now leave the country.

They both grew up in Soviet villages, where they got a good education with the option of going on to college. In those days, graduates were assigned to teach for a few years in the hinterland.

They made fine instructors. Now these women lament the short-age of teachers in their villages, especially competent ones.

Their dreams of combining the best of the Soviet system with new freedoms have not been realized: "Coming to terms with our current reality of corruption and the growing division between rich and poor is hard." They wrestle with why it has turned out so badly, unsure whom to blame. As she urges me to take another cup of tea laced with medicinal honey to fend off my cold, Tamara struggles for an explanation: "I understand there is a war against us, not with weapons, but a kind of spiritual war from the outside perhaps because we are so vulnerable, but we are guilty too because we give in to the worst influences." What worries them most is what they call "moral degradation."

Money is now the key to everything. After-school programs, however limited, were once subsidized. In their place, there is now a huge range of activities, but for a fee. Schools provide no sports programs, so parents drive long distances from neighboring towns to enroll their kids in hockey, soccer, and judo. Girls are now passionate about ballroom dancing and tango, urging their parents to pay for sessions, though a shortage of similarly enthusiastic male partners is evidently a problem. There are also now dozens of cheerleading squads in the Chelyabinsk region. Yes. "Cheerleading" it is indeed called, albeit in accented Russian.

One group I came across practices four hours every day in a rented room inside the run-down former Palace of Culture, deftly avoiding the Soviet chandeliers dripping with dust-covered crystal. Building on Russian expertise in gymnastics, twenty-four girls from seven to eighteen replicate the best they have seen on videos from the United States and Japan, another country with a passion for cheerleading. Their hired coach, Anastastia, wears a T-shirt emblazoned with the English words "SUPER CHEER COACH." One mother, Olga Terzian, the wife of a military officer, is the consummate soccer/cheerleading mom, there every day to help push these girls to flip, lift, and drop each other. As they go through their routines, accented English phrases like "basket toss," "chicken position," "flier," and "catcher" echo in the cavernous hall. Dressed in classic cheerleading outfits, pom-poms and all, they compete at home and abroad and perform at local professional hockey matches to great applause.

Further education, once free for all, is now free for fewer and fewer. Universities now have a complicated system of accepting both students who are funded by the state and those who must pay for themselves. Each department has a different quota system for scholarship students and paid students. Payment varies greatly depending on which field a student chooses. The more attractive fields, like law, business, and administration, have fewer state-funded spots and higher tuitions—even though the shrinking economy means that graduating majors are no longer getting the jobs they once anticipated. With Russia building closer ties to China, the Eurasian departments at Chelyabinsk's universities, where Chinese languages are taught, are quickly becoming the most desirable and expensive.

The introduction of university fees has created a new class of students who feel they can do what they want and that the professors owe them. They appear to have the support of administrators, who often take bribes to accept paying students and then tell professors to do anything necessary to hold on to the cash cows, even if that means tolerating flunking students and cheating. Not surprisingly, professors say the level of higher education is deteriorating.

Several Americans who have taught in Chelyabinsk have been shocked by the amount of outright and shameless cheating. A Fulbright scholar at the Teacher Training University was also stunned by the utter apathy of her students. When she showed them a few TED Talks and asked them what they thought about the issues, they said, "That's not for us to think about. The government, which is wiser than us, will decide."

For young professors, who were excited by the sudden

opportunity in the late 1980s and the 1990s to explore new ideas, this is a devastating reversal. Those who stay at the university say they do it out of passion for their subjects and a few dedicated students. They are certainly not there for the salaries, which are even lower than in secondary schools.

Now in his early thirties, Professor Alexander Hollay, his wife, and two young children live in two small rooms in a dormitory with a communal kitchen and no prospect of moving anywhere else. He teaches chemistry in inadequate facilities and moonlights elsewhere, which cuts into research time. But he loves his profession and thinks it is important for his country's future, even if the government doesn't.

Over six feet tall, long and lean, Hollay calls himself a patriot. He wants his students to cherish what is best about Russia, and he wants his country to be strong enough so that it can make decisions about its destiny without undue pressure from Western financial institutions. In the required course on science, history, and the world he teaches, he explains the reality of globalization. He argues that to defend its interests, Russia needs to be creative and to go beyond its reliance on oil and gas revenue.

■

Hollay is not a fan of the state's continued efforts to control much of the economy. He questions the Kremlin's plans to create what he calls a "fake" Silicon Valley. He, like many whose voices have been ignored, argues you can't order up the brilliance of a Bill Gates or Steve Jobs like food on a menu. Rather, you need to provide incentives for mentors and innovation across the country by encouraging university research facilities and private spin-offs.

Hollay's concerns about Moscow's heavy hand have proved prescient. The plan was to turn Russia, known most for its oil and gas production and its mining of minerals and heavy metals, into an attractive place for homegrown innovation and tech entrepreneurship. The centerpiece was to be the Skolkovo Innovation

Center, a new $4 billion development on a six-hundred-acre plot in a suburb of Moscow. It was to house up to fifty thousand researchers and technology experts. After a promising start, with foreign investors in the wings, the center has had to deal with a climate of corruption, an economic crisis, and cuts in government support. Putin's continued squeeze on Internet freedoms and the free exchange of ideas has put him at further odds with the IT and Web services industry. Foreign investors are wary, and many Russians who had been looking to set up shop in the motherland are today seeking a way out.

At the university, Hollay's lectures include a discussion of what has happened to Russian industry over the past twenty-plus years. He describes how new owners acquired factories for pennies in corrupt auctions and then, because they had no investment, sucked them dry and took their profits out of the country. He tells how he was once hired to help develop a strategic plan for a Chelyabinsk pipe plant, along with Western consulting firms like McKinsey. It was exciting, and all was going well until management decided the effort was too expensive and it could live on what it already did, given then high prices for its raw materials. Those prices have evaporated, and the company now regrets it failed to reform. He tries to tell his students how this shortsighted grab-it-while-it's-there mentality has hurt the country. He tries to tell them how important it is that they all do more than consume. They must also create.

His course got a top rating from a group of bright students I met. But when I asked what they could do to change the status quo, they squirmed. None had been to an opposition protest, and they didn't know anyone who had. They gave the standard line about stability under President Vladimir Putin, though when I asked about their job prospects, they cautiously confessed they were concerned. As early as 2012, though, there were signs that the city's boom, which had lasted more than a decade, was coming to an end. Suddenly Christina, dressed in a fluffy fur vest, thigh-high boots, and a very short miniskirt, broke ranks. "I am sick of rigged elections. We just know who will win, and we can't change it. They get rid of anyone who might challenge Putin. It makes me sad. I don't know what I can do to change things." Her classmates looked away in discomfort.

Christina's English is fluent, buoyed by a summer she spent in the United States on a work-study program, perhaps the most successful of the U.S. State Department's outreach projects. In 2014, amid a paroxysm of anti-Americanism, the Russian government ended its participation in the Future Leaders Exchange program, which brought Russian high school students to the United States to study. But as I write, the Work Travel Program for university students still exists, though a senior professor in town is launching a crusade against it, calling it a U.S. plan to brainwash the best and brightest of Russian students and lure them to stay in the United States.

At its height in 2012, the program granted visas to thirty-two thousand Russian students, including hundreds from remote Chelyabinsk, to come to America for summer jobs and travel. Christina worked as a housekeeper at a Florida resort. She was amazed that Americans did not realize Washington's foreign policy was far from loved overseas. She was struck by American ignorance about the rest of the world and Americans' crude idea that Russia consisted of little more than fat women, dancing bears, eternal winter, and matryoshka nesting dolls. She found that her own ideas about America, though perhaps more informed, were also skewed. As she traveled the country, she was shocked by evidence of poverty and racism, but she also saw a resilience she was unfamiliar with. It wasn't the "We can suffer more than anyone" sensibility she was used to. She came home with a new understanding of what she calls "Russian fatalism": "It comes from our history, from hundreds of years when people were afraid. It's in our blood. We are always waiting for something bad. If something good happens, we are sure something bad will follow. You can't believe in something good in our country. It's only when we go abroad that we relax and see another side." As she spoke to me, her fellow students squirmed even more.

One of her classmates, Dima, has gone on to get a master's in political science and now teaches a course on geopolitics at one of Chelyabinsk's universities. I came across him first when I ordered a taxi. Dima was the driver, making some much-needed extra money.

It was 2014, in the midst of the Ukraine crisis. Chelyabinsk had just held a gubernatorial election, its first since Putin stopped appointing the heads of regions. To add to his paltry salary as a university lecturer, Dima, twenty-five with a baby on the way, conducted some well-paid sociological studies for the regional government in advance of the balloting. He says he is ashamed that he took part in such an utter farce. Putin's appointed governor was running as the unquestionable favorite, and as Dima described it, there was no way for any truly independent candidates to compete. By law, candidates who wished to take part had to get signatures from elected regional officials, almost all of whom were Putin loyalists who won office in rigged elections. The authorities did everything possible to nullify anyone who could even remotely be considered a serious challenger. Those who managed to run got no access to the controlled mainstream media. There were no debates.

Conceding there is now total apathy, Dima says he has no choice but to remain stubbornly optimistic, hoping that people will one day wake up and take a more active role in political and civic life. For now, he says, "The terrible part of our lives is that people hand over responsibility to authorities, believing they know better."

■

There is one area where many students don't let the authorities decide for them, and that's the military draft. Kids at Lyceum 31 were adamant that no one wants to go into the military, calling it "a waste of time." They are sure to get initial exemptions while at college and graduate school. University students are similarly loath to serve when their exemptions expire on graduation.

Russian men are supposed to serve one year, but it's harder and harder to get good recruits because of draft dodging, a fear of hazing, and the demographic crisis of the 1990s. There is a relatively small pool of draft-age young men, and the recent small increase in the birthrate is not going to change that anytime soon. Escaping conscription has become an art form savvy parents start practicing early, slowly building up a convincing medical record so their sons will be rejected. Those who can afford it pay thousands of dollars to doctors to make up imaginary illnesses. Or you can simply bribe a member of the draft board. The going rate in Chelyabinsk is around five thousand dollars. One young man I met didn't even shrug at the prospect of the draft, simply rubbing his fingers together in the well-known sign for money.

The military has been forced to take a lot of marginal, sickly, ill-educated draftees, usually from the countryside, to try to maintain its units. Still, it regularly has 20 percent fewer recruits than it needs. Fulfilling Putin's plans to add yet more military units will be a challenge. This was made clear in remarkably frank public comments from the head of Russia's air force. Of the eleven thousand drafted into the air force in 2011, he said, more than 30 percent were mentally unstable, 10 percent suffered from alcohol and drug abuse, and 15 percent were malnourished. Most come from impoverished villages. The military has contracted a young psychiatrist I met to study why the pool of recruits is so damaged.

Putin is committed to expanding and modernizing the country's military. Indeed, Russia is now engaged in its largest military buildup since the collapse of the Soviet Union more than two decades ago. It has conducted exercises on a scale not seen since the end of the Cold War and according to NATO has regularly violated European airspace. There are plans to pursue a $500 billion rearmament program through 2020. Putin has pushed for this program, even over the objections of some within the Kremlin who worry about costs.

But where is Russia going to get the necessary manpower to fuel this?

And now that the West has cut off credit and access to high-quality components, how can the country's defense industry manufacture the weapons and other tools called for by the new strategy? Attracting much-needed skilled manpower to military plants, which have not had a good reputation, is a challenge. The number of trained engineering and science graduates has plunged in the past two decades, resulting in a frantic competition between old-guard factories and new foreign plants like the United States' Emerson Process Management installation in Chelyabinsk, which produces high-tech monitoring and processing equipment for industry. Now the Russian military is joining the game. At a recent conference in Chelyabinsk, military production facilities proposed a plan that would allow graduates to work for them instead of being drafted. As further inducements, they proposed eliminating their outstanding loans and subsidizing mortgages.

The Russian military has been fighting an image problem that started during the 1980s Afghan war and exploded during the first Chechen war in the mid-1990s. This was a war against a predominantly Muslim region of Russia seeking independence.

Young, untrained draftees were sent into battle without adequate supplies, which had often been stolen by their superiors. When they were killed, their families were sometimes not informed, because officers continued to steal their pay. Their bodies were simply left to rot in the field or were piled up, unidentified, in refrigerated railway wagons. I watched as parents from all over the country came to pick through the corpses, hoping to find their sons who had disappeared without trace.

Attracting conscripts remains a problem to this day—in large part because of the notorious hazing, which ranges from beatings and sexual abuse to torture and in some cases death. Despite years of publicity, human rights activists say they still receive thousands of reports each year, and the incidence appears to be rising, with ethnic minorities often the victims. Dima, the university teaching assistant who was moonlighting as a taxi driver, says hazing is real, not a lie as the military would have it. Of those he knows who served, most saw or experienced it.

The Russian word for military hazing is *dedovshchina*, drawn from the word for "grandfather," Russian slang for older soldiers. Bullying and violence were common in the tsarist army, but ritualized bullying, the so-called grandfather system, emerged in the Soviet army in the 1960s. By then, the better connected were already managing to evade service, and many draftees were recruited from villages and even from prisons. New recruits were made to serve older conscripts in any number of ways. Most of them endured because they had no alternative and no way to protest in those Soviet times. They consoled themselves with the thought they too would be "grandfathers" one day. The system came under fire when Mikhail Gorbachev assumed power. With greater openness, the mothers of soldiers began to speak out about violence and systematized abuse in the Soviet military barracks, and they emerged as a mass movement demanding reforms. In 1990, they claimed that fifteen thousand peacetime or noncombat deaths had occurred in the Soviet armed forces during the preceding four-year period and that the military had covered up those deaths.

The military fought back, accusing "the mothers" of being "unbalanced" and "hysterical" and suggesting they were part of a wider conspiracy to destroy the national defense. But despite efforts to threaten the "mothers" and control press reports, the military was temporarily outmaneuvered by a mass outpouring of maternal grief, growing press freedom, and public outrage. The "mothers" movement grew in the 1990s and continues, though their influence has declined because of exhaustion, increased caution, fear of reprisals, cuts in Western NGO funding, and a reluctance by Russians to fund such a controversial organization (in some regions of the country, the mothers have been labeled "foreign agents").

In Chelyabinsk, two activists have continued the "mothers' movement," renaming it the School for Recruits. The necessity of their work is underscored by the fact that Chelyabinsk has been home to some of the worst and most publicized cases of hazing, with no legal resolution.

On New Year's Eve 2005, eight soldiers were beaten for several hours by their drunken superiors. The nineteen-year-old private Andrei Sychev got the worst of it. His subsequent request for medical help was initially rejected. When he was finally taken to a hospital, he was diagnosed with numerous broken bones and gangrene. Doctors had to amputate his legs and genitals. The military attempted to keep the case from the media and ordered the doctors to keep silent. However, one of the doctors treating Sychev contacted the Committee of Soldiers' Mothers, alerting it and his family of the incident.

In 2010, a freelance journalist named Dayan Shakyovov offered to report on the military during his mandatory service. A Chelyabinsk newspaper waited for his dispatches, but they never arrived. Instead, it received notification that he had committed suicide. His family saw the young soldier's body and reported it was covered in bruises. Their complaints and questions were ignored.

In August 2011, twenty-year-old Ruslan Ayderkhanov went missing from a Chelyabinsk garrison. His body was found hanging from a tree in a nearby woods. When his parents saw massive evidence of beating, they hired the private forensic expert Alexander Vlasov, whose career is described in chapter 14, to investigate. He concluded that the burns, bruises, and broken

bones suggested something other than suicide. Military prosecutors once again closed the case. Some locals believe Ayderkhanov
was killed because he was an ethnic Tatar. Interethnic abuse is
common in the military. It turned out that over a period of six
years, Ayderkhanov was the third conscript from his tiny, predominantly Muslim village of eight hundred to die under highly
suspicious circumstances.

According to Aleksei Tabalov, who heads up the School for
Recruits, a third of all recruits are hospitalized at some point
during their service because of injuries or malnutrition, all the
result of official incompetence or sadistic treatment. The Russian
military has conceded that part of the problem is the absence of a
professional noncommissioned officer corps, the ballast of any
army to maintain discipline and order. Russian conscripts have
been controlled by other conscripts or contract soldiers, with no
effective oversight. Reforms so far have failed to improve this.

■

Like every Russian city, Chelyabinsk has an impressive monument to those who died during World War II. Young couples in
their increasingly elaborate finery go there to pay their respects
and have their increasingly elaborate photographs and videos
taken on their wedding day. The Great Patriotic War, as it's known,
is the last uncontested victory for Russians (as it is for Americans),
and Chelyabinsk's factories and workers played a huge part in
that triumph. The large square with its eternal flame, where
Kolya and Anna left flowers on their wedding day, is a place where
people can feel grateful, sentimental, and proud of their city and
their country. But while veterans from the 1940s are honored,
many soldiers who served afterward, in Afghanistan and Russia's
more recent domestic wars, feel the price they paid was too high
and that they've been ignored.

On a drizzly November day, veterans and soldiers in their
twenties and thirties gathered at the war memorial, less to

celebrate than to commiserate with one another. One counterin-
telligence sergeant who fought in both Chechnya and Dagestan
said, "I don't want to talk about my service," hinting at the terrible things he had seen or done. "I love my country but hate the
government and see no one, no one who can lead us. They gave us
nothing to fight with. You are looking at young men who did it
on their own, with no support, and we came home to nothing. I
would give my life for this country, but this country would do
nothing for my wife and child had I died." Those standing around
him nodded in agreement and took another swig of vodka.

They had gathered for Unity Day, a new holiday that replaces
the once-festive anniversary of the Soviet revolution, with its grand
military marches through Red Square and food packages for
veterans in times of shortage. For all Putin's efforts to promote
national pride, no one quite knows what this Unity Day is all about
or how to mark it. And for these young men, who fought against
fellow Russian citizens in Chechnya and Dagestan, unity has a
hollow ring. They were proud of fighting "enemies of the state"
but traumatized by what they have gone through and bitter
about how they have been treated since.

And there may be a new group of alienated soldiers emerging.
The Russian government has denied its troops are fighting in
eastern Ukraine and does not publicly recognize the growing
number of soldiers and conscripts who have died or been wounded
there. Despite concrete evidence to the contrary, these are usually called victims of training accidents in Russia. So-called volunteers, often military or security forces who take "leaves of
absence," are returning home with mixed stories. Some report being paid extremely well for their service, about which they have
nothing but praise. Others say they were deceived and received
inadequate weapons to fight and little or no pay and were even
forced to steal humanitarian aid sent for civilians. More and more
YouTube videos have surfaced with "volunteers" contradicting
official media reports about the competence of the pro-Russian

fighters they have been sent to support and the prevalence of Ukrainian "fascists" in the ranks of the enemy. Devastated by the destruction they witnessed and the cruelty of the local pro-Russian rebels, some confess they are ashamed they took part in the fighting.

Each soldier and volunteer harbors his own experiences, but there are growing discrepancies between those experiences and the official record. Russia has yet to come to terms with the toll of its open wars in Afghanistan and Chechnya, and it will be years before there is an accurate accounting of this covert operation.

ELEVEN

THE BELIEVERS

In the early 1990s, Chelyabinsk, like the rest of Russia, was flooded with foreign missionaries seeking lost souls. Reforms had unleashed a free market for the nation's hearts and minds. Every possible denomination descended on the country, from Turkish and Arab Muslims targeting Islamic communities to American evangelists who deemed this "godless" industrial wasteland ripe for the picking. For a while, American missionaries attracted impressive audiences. Russians were indeed lost and for a brief moment were happy to look to the West for answers, whether it involved a fast track to God, democracy, or decent living standards.

The Tuesday night show in the former Communist Party theater was definitely not what the Bolsheviks had in mind. It was 1994, and the Seventh-Day Adventists were back for the second year in a row. Alerted by radio ads and posters, 850 people had been coming every night to hear the Americans. For five weeks, it was standing room only. With a full screen flashing photographs and videos behind him and speaking through a translator, Pastor Paul Wolf asked the assembled to show their joy because Christ was coming into their lives. "One more time," he urged, "let's sing 'Jesus Never Fails.'"

The Seventh-Day Adventists established their first congregations in Russia before the revolution, but under Soviet rule they
were banned. Paul Wolf was here to restore the faith. Russians of
all ages sat for three hours on hard seats through a Bible lesson, a
sermon, and a health lecture. He advised the assembled to adopt
a simple diet of grain, fruits, and vegetables. Speaking of the
dangers of too much sugar, he warned, "There was a man in history who loved sugar very much, and his name was Adolf Hitler.
He loved sugar, and that kept him out of balance. You don't want
to be that kind of person." God only knows what Stalin's sugar
intake was.

The rapt audience was also urged to stop smoking, though
after several weeks of counseling only seven of the hundreds in
the hall stood up to say they had quit. Mainly women, they were
invited to come up to the stage, where each was presented with a
tiny American flag. In those days, that seemed cute.

At the end of the evening, the crowd, which was stiff from
sitting so long, shuffled to the foyer to line up for their overcoats.
Some said they were attracted by the direct, simple emotional
message—a stark contrast to the ritual and formality of the Russian Orthodox Church. One forty-year-old man told me he felt
welcome here. He enjoyed the Americans' homey style. He said
everything was understandable, and he liked the fact the Americans dealt with the body as well as the soul. Most, though, were
not ready to commit to any particular church. They had only
recently begun to explore religion and still had many questions.

Those who attended more than ten of the Seventh-Day Ad-
ventist meetings received a free Bible. Many of those Bibles ended
up in the street markets, where desperate Russians were selling
whatever they could. Many Russians came to the American services seeking not only salvation and a Bible but much-needed
medicines, food, and clothing.

In the first years after Communism, the Orthodox Church,
certainly in Chelyabinsk, lost ground. The missionaries were

energetic, and they offered a sense of community. The church, which had collaborated with Soviet power and long been restricted to little more than smoke and incense, was ill-prepared to fight back.

After the Bolshevik Revolution, hundreds of thousands of clergy and believers of all faiths were shot or imprisoned. During and after World War II, some of the remaining religious figures made an uneasy peace with the Communist Party and were allowed to open a very limited number of highly regulated churches. Some churches refused to make a pact and remained underground and under threat. The Orthodox Church, because of its long historic roots, was most useful to the state in its newly harnessed form. Each used the other as necessary. The state permitted services, but not school or community outreach, in a limited number of churches, as well as a handful of seminaries. In return, the church hierarchy supported the atheist state. By dutifully attending international conferences, where it defended Soviet policies including human rights, the church was a useful voice in foreign affairs.

Most church officials were successfully co-opted, but in the 1960s a priest named Gleb Yakunin dared to challenge the Soviet government for restricting religious rights and attacked the leaders of his Orthodox Church for failing to defend those rights. When he spent much of the 1980s in a prison camp and exile, the church did not protest. After the Soviet Union collapsed, Yakunin gained access to KGB archives and published materials that he claimed proved many in the church leadership were KGB agents. The church responded by excommunicating him. With the help of friendly officials, the church has since managed to censor or expunge the records and stop further investigation into its past. Its martyrdom and historic mission is what the Orthodox Church and the Kremlin now want to emphasize.

While foreign interlopers were holding revival meetings, the Orthodox Church set about rebuilding churches, gilding domes, restoring its wealth, and lobbying the increasingly nationalistic government for benefits. The Orthodox Church has been central to Russian identity and empire since 988, when Vladimir the Great made perhaps the most decisive choice in the country's history: he chose to convert pagan Kievan Rus to Byzantium's form of Christianity, rather than Rome's. As a result, Russia had little contact with the humanist currents of the Renaissance. Some have argued that the mystical nature of Orthodox belief, combined with its rigid hierarchy and long alliance with an all-powerful state, helped shape a backward, subservient population. In 1547, Ivan the Terrible was crowned the first tsar of all Russia and announced Moscow to be the "Third and Final Rome," the successor to Saint Peter's Rome and Byzantium, the holiest of holies.

The 1993 Russian Constitution declares there is a separation of church and state and says all religious associations are equal before the law. But over time, the Kremlin and parliament have illegally given preference to what they call the country's four "traditional" religions—Islam, Judaism, Buddhism, and the Orthodox, with the Orthodox Church fighting for and winning distinct advantages. It made a fortune when it was briefly allowed to sell duty-free cigarettes and imported 10 percent of all tobacco into Russia. Other confessions, regardless of how long they have existed in Russia, have often faced outright discrimination.

By the late 1990s, disillusion with the West was growing. Russians wanted to be something more than a poor copy of the West and began searching for a distinctly Russian identity. It was an old impulse, dating back to the nineteenth century, when two movements emerged—Slavophiles, who advocated Russia's unique way of development, and Westernizers, who insisted on the need to join European civilization, with its sociopolitical system, civil society, and culture.

After the first few post-Soviet years, the Orthodox Church, buoyed by new wealth and growing nationalist sentiment, was much better placed to join the fray. The church was once again in bed with the government. As political leaders looked to unify the country, the church was embraced first by Yeltsin, as a counter to his Communist opponents, and then by Vladimir Putin.

When Putin ran for a third term as president in 2012, the Orthodox patriarch Kirill hailed his ascension as "a miracle of God." That statement prompted three members of the all-female punk group Pussy Riot to perform a "blasphemous" prayer in Moscow's central cathedral in which they beseeched the Virgin Mary to rid Russia of Putin. They were convicted of hooliganism "motivated by religious hatred," a charge they denied, and sentenced to two years in a labor camp. They said they were simply protesting against Putin and the church's political interference.

For a brief moment, the harsh verdict opened a debate on the role of the church, its cozy relationship with the Kremlin, and the rule of law, as well as Western influences. While applauded by Moscow liberals and many in the West, Pussy Riot did not get overwhelming support elsewhere. Most Russians were uncomfortable with their style and methods, and many bought into the Kremlin's charges that they were paid agents of the West.

Other incidents involving the church simultaneously hit the newsstands. There were embarrassing stories about the scale and luxury of the patriarch's private accommodations. Then a blogger published a photograph that showed him wearing a thirty-thousand-dollar Breguet watch. His press office had airbrushed the watch out of the photograph on the church's Web site. It might have gotten away with the gambit but for one mistake: it had failed to erase the watch's reflection, which was clearly visible on the polished table where the patriarch was sitting.

For Roman, the plastic-pane manufacturer, this just reinforced his belief that the Orthodox Church is once again little more than a corrupt government asset. He looks for different manifestations of patriotism and pride, ideally based on the rule of law and a sense of civic duty. The Chelyabinsk historian

Vladimir Bozhe warns of problems to come. He says the tragedy of the Orthodox Church has always been that it gets too close to the state—and then pays a price for it. When the tsarist state failed in the years leading up to the 1917 revolution, the Orthodox Church failed with it; then the church made a pact with the new rulers, whom it now calls Communist devils.

Controversy over the actions of church leaders has put little dent in its standing, though Putin's efforts to use the Orthodox Church have had mixed results. According to polls, as many as two-thirds of ethnic Russians now say they are Orthodox believers, though many of these same people also say they don't actually believe in God. It is popular to be baptized and wear crosses. At the same time, it was clear at several adult baptism classes I attended that those present had little or no understanding of the tenets of the church; they were there out of tradition, patriotism, or a raw mysticism. Only a tiny fraction of the population—5 to 10 percent—attend services or do more than light a candle. The church still feels vulnerable, especially to what it calls "unhealthy" Western influence. A professor at one of Chelyabinsk's universities asked a class how many were believers. Out of forty students, about half put up their hands, but of those almost none could name the four evangelists. Summing up, he noted, "Their knowledge was slim. Russian belief is very peculiar."

President Putin has to walk a fine line with the Orthodox Church, relying on it when it is useful but distancing himself when he needs to appeal to Russia's minorities, especially Russia's large and growing Muslim population. He alternates between stressing Russia's holy roots and calling Russia a multi-confessional country. He talks passionately, if vaguely, of patriotism and spiritual values to be drawn from Russia's past. He has repeatedly urged the nation to look for guidance in Russian historical traditions, not in Western political models.

Nina Timofeevna, a fifty-seven-year-old accountant, is confused by her country's history as it is written, rewritten, and fought over. For her, Putin's search for roots just doesn't cut it. She is not at all sure what ideals she should learn from the past. She misses the surety of Soviet patriotism that she grew up with, but she can no longer draw on that and doesn't want to return to that past. Casting about for something positive, she finds solace not in the church but in people, their capacity for resilience, great friendship, and hospitality. She loves her country's stunning landscape. She says, "It is quite simply my motherland." She, like so many Russians, resorts to the celebrated verse of the Romantic poet Fyodor Tyutchev:

> *Russia cannot be known by the mind*
> *Nor measured by the common mile:*
> *Her status is unique, without kind—*
> *Russia can only be believed in.*

Chelyabinsk has been relatively tolerant of other creeds, in part because it has a large Muslim minority and in part because, as one Orthodox priest put it, "Chelyabinsk with its military plants and Soviet industry was a dead zone for the church."

The first post-Soviet Orthodox archbishop in Chelyabinsk was neither active nor forceful. His replacement, Archbishop Feofan, was appointed with the specific task of raising up the church and expanding its presence. A small man with a scruffy white beard and the required long hair, he is tough, wily, media savvy, and politically adroit. He set up a PR department and organized regular TV programs, an outlet other faiths are denied. He put more emphasis on social programs. He quickly took over a prime building, with help from the government, to open a church school. He started an addiction center; so far, it's a weak challenge to the Evangelicals in an area where they had made inroads.

The main cathedral in Chelyabinsk has been restored with glistening golden domes. The interior crackles with devotional candles lit in front of icons and the hint of incense from the morning service. In an interview, Archbishop Feofan was emphatic that the Orthodox Church must be the country's unifying force, a boost to flagging patriotism, and the inspiration for a renewal of tradition and values. Despite the constitution, he echoes the patriarch, making it quite clear he does not believe all religions should be on an equal footing. "If religions don't contradict society, let them exist, but that doesn't mean they should immediately have the status of a religion that has existed here for more than a thousand years." He has pushed for all regional schools to have a course in Orthodox history and culture. No such attention would be given other confessions, especially indigenous Muslims, whose roots precede the establishment of Orthodoxy and who make up at least 14 percent of the local population.

Feofan has little patience for those who believe the intimacy of the church and the state violates the constitution. In fact, he would like to see even better relations, with the church enjoying exclusive state patronage. "I think the government should invest in the church's social and education activities, as well as the restoration of cathedrals and churches," he says. And indeed, it appears he has succeeded in persuading the local government to help pay for at least a dozen new churches. The response to the funding has not been altogether positive—with taxpayers raising concerns on the Internet that the government can ill afford this.

Feofan deftly dodges questions about church corruption, including reports that his sixtieth birthday celebration cost $500,000. He simply says that "people are generous." He will not discuss the church's questionable past, casting the church as Communism's victim while ignoring the suffering of other confessions. As he sees it, the Soviet attempt to destroy the country's traditions and a generation of Orthodox leaders led to the destruction of a great country. For him, the resurrection of the church means the resurrection of Russia.

Father Dmitri Yegorov, a young priest in the outlying town

of Chebarkul, agrees that the fates of the church and Russia are inextricably intertwined. Yet while he delights in seeing the gilded domes rise again, he also believes that priests must lead by example and do much more to support and engage the community. He lives modestly with three children in a two-room apartment even as he combats accusations of high living and corruption in the church.

His new church, built on the foundations of one destroyed in 1937, overlooks the lake where a large chunk of the meteor sank. Old women, the gatekeepers of every Orthodox church, where they typically chastise visitors for doing something wrong, welcome and instruct. There is an unusual, and unusually well-attended, Sunday school where fathers play chess with their sons, and girls and their mothers learn how to make intricate Christmas decorations. There is a library with volunteers ready to help and a teen group who watch videos and discuss them. There is a new refuge for those fleeing abuse, alcoholism, and drugs, though it has no professional support. Father Dmitri also works as the chaplain at the local military barracks, where he deals with interethnic conflict between Russian Muslims and others, as well as general despondency and despair. "We can't force someone to be Orthodox, though I believe that is the true religion. I can tell young soldiers to get an education and work for the country and fight what you don't like." He starts with baby steps: "Stop swearing, stop smoking, and before you throw trash on the street, stop and think. It's a beginning." He won't say where they should move on to from there.

Father Dmitri works with the mosque in his town, but he has nothing to do with the other Christian confessions. He says, "Orthodoxy is our roots, the roots from which our country evolved, and it is a mistake for us to search out something new."

The Orthodox Church, gaining in power, has increasingly fueled discrimination against other Christian denominations by calling them "un-Russian foreign sects" (the word "sect" being a deliberately pejorative term). Pentecostals, Mormons, and Jehovah's

Witnesses have come in for particular attack. Patriarch Kirill has said that unlike in the United States, there can be no place in Russia for a free market in religious life. He has called foreign missionary activity a sinister threat to the nation's security. In certain regions, the Orthodox Church has quietly used its authority to prevent "nontraditional" communities from registering with the government, which is a legal requirement. Despite constitutional guarantees, the Orthodox Church has used "telephone justice," or informal pressure, to get sympathetic regional officials to create obstacles for competing confessions.

Religious life in the Chelyabinsk region has remained surprisingly diverse if not entirely free. Jews, members of one of the four "traditional faiths," reopened their synagogue in 1992, though their numbers have fallen due to emigration and assimilation. The synagogue has been taken over and restored by the ultra-Orthodox Chabad Lubavitchers. Despite their shallow roots here, they are now the dominant Jewish force in Russia. They have been ardent Putin supporters. The local Chabad rabbi, Meir Kirsh, came to Chelyabinsk from Brooklyn speaking not a word of Russian. He found a Jewish community wherein almost no one spoke Hebrew or Yiddish. The number of those attending the synagogue has dropped from a high of five hundred to two hundred or so on a high holy day and only a handful the rest of the time. With his black hat and long beard, marks of Hasidic tradition, Rabbi Kirsh has turned away or turned off a lot of people—not that he seems concerned. Following Orthodox law, he says those whose mothers are not Jewish are not Jews, even if the Soviets classified them that way and they suffered for it, and even if they see themselves as Jews today. He does not encourage conversion and has supervised only one in all the years he has been here.

■

Mormons, a new import, have succeeded in renting space on the fourth floor of an office building where a Sunday service draws about thirty people, down from a few years ago. There are eight missionaries, mainly Americans, with little to show for their years here. The mission president, E. Kent Rast, says that in six months, over a huge swath of territory in central Russia, they have baptized seven people, equal to what Mormon missionaries would expect to achieve in a day in Brazil. Russia has been a much greater challenge than expected. Mormon missionaries say the good news is that in Chelyabinsk they only get hassled, while their brothers and sisters have been threatened and beaten up in other Russian cities. Given the country's growing nationalism, Mormons would like to cut back on American missionaries and rely more on Russians. Native speakers would be more acceptable messengers, but their numbers remain small.

After the Orthodox, the most numerous Christian groups are Catholics, Lutherans, Adventists, and Evangelicals, though they are not nearly as successful as they anticipated in the 1990s. Though they existed in Russia before the revolution, they have not been included in the list of "four traditional faiths." Many who historically belonged to these churches were immigrants from Germany or other European countries. A Baptist missionary once told me, "We were naive, understanding neither how unacceptable we are to most Russians nor the strength of the Orthodox Church, which is part of the unconscious of the people."

As we've seen, evangelical churches were quick to set up much-needed addiction rehab centers and halfway houses, drawing many in their congregations from the wounded and those who wanted to help. But their efforts to extend such programs to hospitals and prisons have been blocked. A Baptist pastor, Vitaly Sobolev, was told by the local authorities, " 'We have an arrangement with the Orthodox Church,' and that was the end of the discussion"—though this violates the law. Sobolev has to continually battle Orthodox charges that his church is a "foreign un-Russian sect," but he treads carefully, saying, "If we are too active, too loud, I am sure there would be problems." He adds, "We understand the need to be prudent."

In 2014, as anti-Americanism grew, two Pentecostal missionaries from Madison, Wisconsin, a married couple with three children and minimal Russian, nonetheless received visas to serve in Chelyabinsk. They were careful about their work, using free English classes, rather than street proselytizing, as a way to bring more people to the church.

The Wisconsin missionaries have worked closely with the pastor at the Word of God Church. He has long ties with America, and a child studying at a Bible college there, but the missionaries still see a growing anti-Americanism among the congregation. Despite the state's poor treatment of so-called nontraditional religions, they have been stunned by the local Evangelicals' support for Vladimir Putin, his takeover of Crimea, and Russia's efforts to maintain its influence in Ukraine. The American missionaries steer clear of politics. Their goal is to strengthen the selection of pastors and help with church activities without micromanaging them. Ultimately, they hope to "plant" a new church in St. Petersburg.

A longtime friend is a member of the Word of God Pentecostal church, which shares space with other evangelical communities at the same former Communist theater I visited more than two decades ago. At its appointed hour—10:00 a.m. on a Sunday—Ruta Vericheva and her family join more than a hundred others to sway to the energetic hymns performed by the rock band on the stage. The words are broadcast on large screens. Ruta would like to open a new church in her own village, a half hour from the city, but the local authorities have made it clear such a move would not be welcome.

Nearly six feet tall, with long streaked hair pulled back in a clip, Ruta could be mistaken for a model. By 2000, she says, she was in really bad shape. Her husband, once a world champion in judo, was killing himself with booze. He was a local star, a charmer who didn't know what else to do once his winning streak was over. She drank with him and their crowd until they lost everything. It was the birth of their daughter that shook her out of her alcoholic stupor. She tried to leave her husband, and when his threats didn't deter her, he had his buddies in the police force threaten her. She went into hiding. Then by a fluke she ended up taking a friend's place on an exchange program to the United States sponsored by the State Department. The ostensible goal was to learn about business development. She pursued her interest in landscape design and gardening. She also found God.

Brought up in the Soviet Union, and with only the vaguest notion about religion, she thought the only Christians were Russian Orthodox. Her American hosts in Louisiana gave her a Bible and religious films in Russian. She went to church with them, and when she returned to Chelyabinsk, she started attending the local Baptist church. Her first husband died of alcohol poisoning. She met and married a recovering alcoholic through her church, and together she and Igor have built up a successful landscape business.

They bought cheap land in a village about thirty miles outside the city. The former state farm had gone bankrupt, and the area was little more than a trash heap. Bit by bit, they started to grow plants to supply their business. She and Igor have depended on a few wealthy clients who want instant gardens, with perennial beds, fountains, orchards, and woodlands dotted with fully grown trees and shrubs. To satisfy their customers, they bought more cheap land in the Siberian taiga where they can cultivate fir trees, which are not native to Chelyabinsk but very much in demand. They built their own house, room by room, floor by floor. It's now a comfortable place where the hallway, full of tiny boots and parkas, shows evidence of several children. In addition to the daughter by her first marriage, Ruta and Igor have had a son. They have also adopted two little girls.

Ruta describes how four years ago she was taken to the gates of Ozersk, the closed nuclear weapons city, where two siblings were up for adoption. She was not permitted to enter the fenced-in city for security reasons. The children were brought out to her, and she was told, in front of the two girls, "Take them now or forget it." She could not make such a decision on the spot without consulting her husband, and so she declined—and wept all the way home. They subsequently took in two other sisters. The kitchen-living area is full of dolls and Legos, as well as a wide-screen TV. Serviced by a satellite dish, they watch only Christian programming.

Ruta first took classes at the Baptist church, as well as local seminars, on "self-realization." She and Igor also completed a two-year Internet Bible course through an American college based in California. Once they were more or less settled, Ruta decided it was time to help people who had gone through what they had. "We knew there was a way out and we could help, not just get people off drugs and alcohol, but let them be full people and full members of society."

They started a rehab center in a tiny outbuilding with enough room to house four people at a time. Like the larger fundamentalist church-based programs, it is voluntary and based on prayer and Bible study. Those who come to her for help also work in the gardens to pay for their food, housing, and care. Most drop out of the program. Those who have made it through often stay on in the area working for Ruta and Igor as fully salaried employees.

The first to enter their program was Elena, who is now an unofficial member of the family. Petite, with long dark hair, she arrived five years ago, looking more like a frightened mouse than the self-confident twenty-eight-year-old she has become. She had worked in a factory in a local city, earning a pittance. She says everyone around her drank or took drugs. She fell into the same pattern and gradually succumbed to despair. A friend told her about Ruta and Igor. "I came here, and my life has changed," she says. Thanks to Ruta, and her work in the landscape business,

Elena has recently been on a three-week bus tour of Europe. She owns a car. Now she would like to find a decent guy.

At Ruta's fortieth birthday party, friends from across the years gathered at the house. There was no alcohol, and when a member of her church broke out his guitar and started playing hymns, with Ruta taking the lead in a soft soprano, some of the guests from her earlier life were clearly uncomfortable. Ruta suddenly burst out laughing at her religious passion, her long manicured fingers fluttering as she spoke. "I love God," she whispered to me, "and I can talk about him all the time. I can't keep my mouth shut, though my daughter thinks I am nuts."

The local villagers also think she and Igor are pretty strange. Ridiculous rumors have circulated that they are members of a satanic sect that sacrifices children. Until recently, Ruta ignored politics, but unlike many in her church she is increasingly concerned about the direction her country is taking. Given her family's distant roots in the Baltic States, she is thinking of buying land there and possibly emigrating.

TWELVE

THE MUSLIM
COMMUNITY

On New Year's Eve 1994, I was caught in Grozny, the capital of Chechnya, a southern Russian republic in the Caucasus. Russian tank columns were moving in to crush a bid for independence. This predominantly Muslim region had fought off tsarist forces for more than a century before it was finally conquered in 1862. Resistance and brutal repression continued. With the breakup of the Soviet Union, Chechnya once again sought to separate from Moscow. I took refuge in a basement as Chechen defenders I had come to know—teachers, doctors, factory workers, and farmers—battled in the streets above. They figured they didn't have a chance against the overwhelming Russian force, but they decided to make a valiant, honorable last stand, expecting defeat and a quick end to their separatist dream. They were lightly armed and fought back with homemade Molotov cocktails. The invasion was so badly organized, and the Russian soldiers so ill equipped and trained, that much to their surprise the Chechens destroyed the first tank columns that entered the city.

In the dawn when I emerged, there was carnage. Charred Russian soldiers lay on the roadsides. Their tanks, caught up in the narrow streets, had been burned to a crisp, often by friendly fire. One lone tank forced into a corner frantically swung its turret in desperate circles, until the crew gave up. They were treated well.

The war dragged on. The Russian military adopted more and more brutal tactics, including indiscriminate bombing. The Chechens responded in kind. What started out as a nationalist Chechen fight for independence acquired more and more religious overtones as radical Islamists took control, fueled in part by foreign Muslims who joined the battle.

After a stalemate and an uneasy peace marked by dramatic, bloody attacks by Chechen insurgents on civilian targets, the war resumed when Vladimir Putin became president in 2000. This time, Moscow largely crushed the Chechen revolt, leveling the capital, which had once been home to half a million people. It eventually installed the former rebel Ramzan Kadyrov as a Russian puppet and basically gave him the right to do anything he pleased regardless of the constitution, as long as he kept semipeace. He instituted his own version of Muslim law to counter the insurgents. A repressive dictatorship, rampant corruption, and egregious human rights violations were the price Moscow was willing to pay to establish, if not total peace, then control. With the destruction of much of the region and the deaths of tens of thousands of Chechens, the population is exhausted and terrified. It may be quiet now, but the fate of Chechnya is far from decided.

The Chechen rebel leadership has gone underground with the goal of creating an Islamic caliphate across Russia's North Caucasus region. The insurgency has spread to the neighboring Muslim republics of Dagestan, Ingushetia, and Kabardino-Balkaria. This is the poorest area of Russia, a region where people are disillusioned by unemployment of catastrophic proportions and widespread corruption. The extreme measures Moscow has used have only increased religious extremism. The indiscriminate arrest and torture of young men, who often disappear while in custody, is driving more recruits into the ranks of fighters, known as "going to the forest." Families of suspected insurgents are also often punished, their houses destroyed. Increasingly, people in the region fear Moscow's security forces more than they do the insurgents.

What does this have to do with Chelyabinsk, hundreds of miles away in central Russia? More and more, a great deal. The Urals region has a significant indigenous Muslim minority made up of the Bashkirs and Tatars who lived here long before Russian colonists arrived in the eighteenth century. They have been joined by Muslims fleeing the conflict in the North Caucasus as well as Muslims migrating here from the former Soviet Muslim republics of central Asia just to the south of Chelyabinsk.

Like Russia's Orthodox Christians, these Muslims are experiencing a cultural and religious revival, and the Kremlin is terrified that the radicalism now evident in southern regions is moving here. Its efforts to deal with this are inept, haphazard, heavy-handed, and for now effective, but they have left brewing resentment.

The Kremlin sends totally contradictory messages. It gives huge advantages to the Orthodox Church, citing it as the source of the nation's spiritual strength and tradition, while in the next breath extolling a multi-confessional, multiethnic population. This does not go down well with Russia's minorities. And the Orthodox Church in Chelyabinsk risks exacerbating tensions by building more and more churches at illegal state expense, while those already open are far from full. It wants to impose Orthodox education in the schools. But Muslim villages desperately in need of mosques and social services get little.

Traditionally, Russian Muslims have been Sunni adherents of the moderate Hanafi and Shafi'i schools of religious law. There are also many Sufis. Under the Soviet authorities, Muslim religious leaders, such as they were, were compliant and conformist, what the Kremlin calls "traditional." Religious education was limited, and Islam to a large degree was reduced to a folk culture. With greater freedom, there has been access to new ideas. Many are raising questions about what it means to be a Muslim in this day and age. Given the rise of extremism around the world and a Muslim insurgency in Russia's south, these questions, however benign, are highly threatening for both the Kremlin and Russia's ill-educated "traditional" Muslim leadership.

The country's state-registered Muslim authorities generally get little loyalty from ordinary Muslims. Their religious credentials are dubious, as is their adherence to basic Islamic principles. Many drink and smoke. They are generally lumped together with corrupt officials out for power and money, and their venality and intrigues have alienated many young Muslims.

The Kremlin has given particular support to the most subservient and craven of the Muslim organizations, which fight among themselves and call any and all competitors extremists. The bottom line is that the government believes there is good Islam, loyal to the state, and "bad" Islam, a creature of foreign forces aimed at destabilizing the country. In their effort to control the process of Islamic revival, officials have relied on co-opting the Muslim leadership and discrediting or arresting those who hold "nontraditional" views. This black-and-white approach isn't working very well.

For the most part, the Muslim renaissance in Chelyabinsk consists of an easygoing search for roots and pride in ethnic and religious identity. At the White Mosque, shuttered by Stalin and reopened in the 1990s, an old man sits at an old desk in a side office with a couple of chairs. Petitioners wait in line. They stuff rubles into a box before he mumbles prayers for family troubles, deaths, or anniversaries. He has no religious education. A young man rushes in and drops off some cash for a quick blessing because there is going to be a Tatar night at a local disco where ethnic Tatar men hope to meet Tatar women. When I ask him about details, he advises me to come before 11:00 p.m. Otherwise, he says, everyone will be drunk. The old man, saying the prayers, merely chuckles.

Rinat Rayev, a former veterinarian, is the head mufti at the mosque and presides over many of the region's outlying Muslim communities, a source of money and power. A large photograph of President Vladimir Putin, wearing a skullcap, dominates his office. Rayev has built his reputation on loyalty to the state and warnings about dangerous, radical "nontraditional" influences. In a Friday sermon in the run-up to the last presidential elections, he told his congregation to vote for United Russia, the Kremlin's party, and for Putin.

The mosque is centrally located and conveniently just down the street from the Federal Security Service headquarters. By noon on Fridays, the courtyard fills with men waiting for the start of prayer. They stand in small groups, local Bashkirs, Tatars, and migrants from elsewhere, separated by ethnicity and suspicion. It's widely understood that undercover cops are somewhere in the crowd, listening in and watching.

Thirty-year-old Abdul says he tries to ignore the cops, and Mufti Rayev too. He believes Rayev serves the state, not religion. Rayev, he complains, says what he has to say and not what people need to hear. Abdul comes here because it's close to his business in a neighboring park. His focus is on Allah and prayer.

With his dark hair and skin and heavy beard, Abdul is immediately identifiable as "foreign." He moved here to escape the tumult in his native Dagestan, a southern region next to Chechnya, but though a Russian citizen, he is regularly hassled. It's not as bad as Moscow, where police constantly stop "foreign"-looking men, but it's not great. Abdul says he has had to move apartments several times because of trumped-up complaints by neighbors who don't want someone like him in their building.

The irony is that Abdul served in the Russian military for eight years, fighting Islamic extremists in Chechnya and Dagestan.

When we first met, insurgents had just put out a death warrant for him on YouTube, accusing him of being a traitor to Islam. The video included his photograph as well as his family's address in Dagestan. YouTube eventually blocked the threatening post.

After eight years, Abdul finally left the military because he was told he would not be promoted due to his ethnicity and religion: "My commander put me in for an award, but I was turned down, and he confessed it was because I had the wrong last name. He said he couldn't do anything, and that was the last straw. I resigned."

Abdul had joined the military after his aunt was killed by insurgents. He said he thought he was defending the motherland, but slowly his attitude began to change when he saw how Russian forces operated and how he was discriminated against. He was also disgusted by the corruption among the officers, which left him and his soldiers without the means to fight. He says that he wanted to serve Russia but that Russia has betrayed him.

Abdul is caught in the middle, but he admits he is now better able to understand the views of the very insurgents who want to kill him. "I am not happy with the way the government is handling ethnic problems," he says. Referring to the frequent disappearance of young men in the North Caucasus and the punishment of family members as a deterrent, he asks, "Why do they kill suspects and destroy their family houses without any investigation?" Unless the government changes its policies, he anticipates greater problems between the North Caucasus and Russia. "Our attitudes to Russian power are getting worse," he warns.

As we talk in whispers in the dubious safety of my apartment, there is a knock at the door. Two polite policemen are there, alerted by someone that "a foreigner" is living in the building. In this case, the "foreigner" in question appears to be me. I am disconcerted, but Abdul is terrified, and while their attention is focused on me, he slips out. That will be our last meeting.

The city of Chelyabinsk is predominantly ethnic Russian,

but once you cross its boundaries, you come upon indigenous Tatar and Bashkir villages. Bazhikaeva is predominantly Bashkir, though at first glance there's nothing to set it apart from any other Russian village. There is a hint of Asian influence in some people's faces, but that's not a sure way to establish who is Bashkir and who isn't. The Bashkir clothing doesn't set them apart from others. The housing could be anywhere in Russia—the ubiquitous simple wood structures or the stark one-story white-brick houses from Soviet times. Those houses are typically divided to accommodate two families. The fortunate have running water, with the rest relying on outdoor plumbing. Beside most houses are sheds thrown together with wooden slats for livestock and yards full of haystacks for feed and stacks of wood for heat. Cows, geese, and ducks wander the dirt paths.

There is no mosque in Bazhikaeva, so Rafit Bayaditov's fifty-fifth birthday celebration takes place at home, overseen by a respected old man who has been hired as an unofficial mullah for the occasion. Seventy-eight-year-old Khrikmat Izatullin learned the prayers from his parents in secret and only openly professed his faith twenty years ago. With everyone seated at a long table, he gently sings in lilting Arabic what he memorized long ago as a child.

Rafit Bayaditov, the birthday boy, was a local Communist Party member and village official and flashes his party card to prove it. He only recently began to believe in God, exclaiming with the passion of a convert, "I love the changes. What has happened is for the best. We have our Bashkir language back, and our history." He cuts a doughnut into two unequal parts. Lifting the smaller portion, he says, "This is what we knew about the world," then, taking up the larger one, he says, "This is what we know now."

The men, wearing skullcaps for the celebration, sit at one end of the table, with the women, wrapped in colorful scarves, at the other. Rafit's daughter, a well-educated professional who now lives in the city, dutifully works the rudimentary kitchen with other young female relatives, summoning soups as if by magic. She passes a bowl of water. First the men, then the women wash their hands three times. The table is loaded with cakes, cookies, and steaming kettles. No alcohol is served, but once the mullah has left, the vodka will be broken out. One guest after another distributes coins to other guests, a wish for future prosperity. Specially composed birthday poems are recited in Bashkir. The older women flash smiles of gold or missing teeth. The younger ones show the results of the improved dentistry that is available in the surrounding towns at a price. The conversation about how so much has changed in Rafit's lifetime flips back and forth between Russian and Bashkir, with guests from the city now more comfortable speaking Russian. The women ask me if I like Danielle Steel and Jackie Collins, their favorite writers readily available in translation. They gobble up details about American life. It's a bit disconcerting to think their impressions come from these sole sources.

Bazhikaeva is typical. The local collective farm fell apart when economic reforms were implemented, forcing people to fend for themselves. The young try to leave. Pensioners get by on what they grow in their gardens. The school hasn't been able to find teachers, and the clinic has struggled without a doctor. The elderly are often told they should not expect anything more than a few pills. Rafit's son-in-law Ruslan, who is working to improve the lot of Bashkirs, says limited educational opportunities and the high cost of college are serious problems and must be addressed so that the Bashkirs can play a greater role in regional politics, where they are dramatically underrepresented.

All the local Bashkir and Tatar villages are struggling to move out of poverty. What sets Arga apart is a tiny mosque. On a rise, tucked into a birch grove, a shiny green minaret pokes through the trees. Inside there is a small alcove where women prepare a Bashkir lamb soup on hot plates to be served after the Friday service. The mosque is essentially one room divided lengthwise by green and pink nylon curtains, one side for women and the other for men. A ragged assortment of rugs covers the floor, though in the absence of any heat they do little to block the rising chill. The assembled, perhaps twenty in all and most on the far side of fifty, are bundled up, with old-fashioned felt boots the preferred defense against frozen feet. The young are away at work, bused to mines and factories in the area. But on Saturday mornings, many of them come to the mosque for classes.

With the support of the community, seventy-five-year-old Marcel Istamgulov, a former tractor operator at the now-defunct collective farm, has assumed the role of local imam. He leads the prayers with what little he has been able to memorize from the Koran. He speaks about a Muslim's obligation to make a pilgrimage to Mecca and then introduces a young man who's just returned from the hajj to describe his experience. Despite the expense for these poor farmers and pensioners, at least seven in the village have now made the trip, with more in the area hoping to go each year.

There is a shortage of trained Muslim clerics, especially in villages like Arga. Istamgulov is totally self-taught. He does what he can to encourage people to return to their faith and live by Islamic law, emphasizing a ban on alcohol. "You know what it has done to our villages," he says. He enlisted a local farmer, thirty-year-old Vilyard Yakupov, to give occasional evening and Saturday classes in the Arabic language and the fundamentals of Islam.

Yakupov grew up here with absolutely no knowledge of his background or Islam. His family had been totally Russified, and he was smart enough to get into a military school in the regional capital. One day, when he was nineteen, he describes hearing a call to prayer. It was 1998. He asked his friends what "that screaming was." "It's your church," a Christian friend told him. "They do it every day." During a break, he went to see what was going on. He was intrigued and kept going back.

In the early twenty-first century, Yakupov spent two years

studying Arabic in Saudi Arabia on a Saudi scholarship. In those days, the Saudis were allowed to support the community, though Yakupov believes the local Muslim leadership managed to steal most of the investment.

Given the low level of Islamic education in Russia following years of Soviet restrictions, many Muslims went abroad to study when the borders to the outside world first opened in the 1990s. The government now discourages this. The Kremlin, as well as some of the Soviet-educated Muslim leadership, suspects these students of bringing back "nontraditional" ideas that could fuel growing radicalism.

The Kremlin's Muslim problem has been played out in this tiny village. Vilyard Yakupov was charged with spreading extremist views, a criminal offense, and became a pawn in a vicious fight involving Russia's competing Muslim authorities, local politics, and the security services' hunt for radical Islamists. For three years, accusations, searches, manipulation of the law, and power plays terrified and divided the community and served as a warning to others.

Yakupov, who wears a modest beard, doesn't hesitate to shake my hand when we meet. He says he wants his daughters to get an education. "It is up to them how they develop," he tells me. "I found my way, and they will find theirs." There is little in our many interviews that suggests he is an Islamic extremist. He is a devout Muslim and an innovative farmer, and he believes his troubles started when he backed an independent candidate in local elections—a candidate, he is quick to point out, who was not an observant Muslim, let alone an extremist. He describes himself as a talented, honest farmer who could help the area develop. Yakupov watched as the elections were hijacked by ballot stuffing, and he protested. Along with this, he supported the construction of local mosques, independent of the Kremlin's favored Muslim organizations. All this brought him into the cross hairs of the local authorities, the Kremlin's favored mosque, and the security services.

Yakupov was denounced by Rinat Rayev, the leading Muslim cleric sixty miles away in Chelyabinsk. Yakupov apparently got in his way by questioning his religious credentials, his conduct, and his push to control the Muslim communities and their finances. Rayev told the authorities that Yakupov had called for the overthrow of Christianity and the installation of Saudi rule. According to his official deposition, Rayev offered no evidence to support this, other than Yakupov's period of study in Saudi Arabia. Yakupov denied the charges, calling them absurd. The elderly village imam Marcel Istamgulov also denied them. In fact, no one in the village who knew Yakupov or attended his classes could be found to confirm the charges. But the FSB did cite the testimony of two of its own drivers who claimed Yakupov had tried to subvert them and get them to join a terrorist organization. In subsequent interviews, their relatives admitted they had been pressured. The FSB then swept in to search the mosque and Yakupov's house. It confiscated large quantities of books and printed materials and, without reading any of it, immediately alleged that it was extremist literature. The message was clear. The enemy had infiltrated even here, the far reaches of Russia.

To combat extremism of all kinds, the government has developed a list of "inflammatory" publications and banned them. Even a very junior court, relying on questionable expertise, can rule materials "extremist," obliging Moscow to include them on the federal list. Any work deemed to incite hatred can end up on the list, from neo-Nazi and ultranationalist literature to tracts by Jehovah's Witnesses and Scientologists. But the ban has focused most of all on Islamic books, which in some cases have been outlawed for claiming Islam is the one true religion. Most religions claim this. The catechism of the Orthodox Church declares its supremacy over all other religions.

Alexey Malashenko, a leading expert on Russian Islam, has said, "It is stupid to prohibit all these books," arguing, "If you ban the life of Sheikh Ibn 'Abd al-Wahhab, the founder of

Saudi-based fundamentalist Wahhabism, then you must prohibit all of Lenin's books and articles immediately since they too discriminate against classes of people." Malashenko says, "The problem is not the books but how they are used."

Mufti Rayev, on whose deposition much of the case against Yakupov rested, ignored repeated demands he appear in court to face the defense, though he was never held accountable for his repeated and unexplained absence. While the case dragged on for three years, Yakupov was ordered to stay in the village, with no way to sell his produce, buy new seeds, or otherwise conduct business to support his wife and four children. When all was said and done, only two of the hundreds of books in Yakupov's possession were found to be on the banned list. One was a study of Sharia law. Two of three experts brought in said there was no basis for the book's prohibition, but Yakupov was convicted of inciting hatred and fined the equivalent of five thousand dollars. "If I had advocated or tried to overthrow the government, I should have been arrested," Yakupov told me, "but my sin was merely discussing religion."

Once Yakupov had been convicted, Mufti Rayev was invited to town by the mayor and found time to visit the village. A town meeting was held in the local drinking and disco club, an insult to observant Muslims if not to Rayev. Rayev once again warned the villagers about extremists in their midst. An uproar ensued. Imam Istamgulov and others called Rayev the extremist for creating religious and racial tensions and unfounded fears. Rayev and the security services succeeded in dividing the community and scaring many away from the mosque, but he has so far failed to take it over. "What right does he have to come here and threaten us? What right does he have to interfere in our mosque, since we don't belong to him?" Istamgulov asks. "And what right does the mayor have to get involved with religion and our mosque, which is legal and which we, its members, paid for?"

I sat with Yakupov and a group of local farmers after a Friday service, trying to sort this all out. Their explanation is that the mayor wanted Rayev and his organization to take over the mosque because Yakupov and Istamgulov, a member of the village council, had raised uncomfortable questions about corruption and mismanagement. They assume Yakupov was easy prey because he had studied in Saudi Arabia and was therefore suspect. His arrest would be a boon for law enforcers eager to show they had captured feared radicals.

Yakupov insists he is a loyal citizen of Russia, with many Christian relatives. He says the witch hunt for fanatics only alienates Muslims who are pursuing questions of social justice and Islam's role in their lives. He also avows that Rayev's alignment with the security services and his fealty to the state render him incapable of answering young Muslims' concerns. Over the course of many months, I repeatedly asked Mufti Rinat Rayev for an interview. He never returned my calls.

Yakupov, along with many Russian experts, believes the government's heavy-handed approach may be creating the very extremism it is trying to curb. He cites its decision to ban Hizb ut-Tahrir, an international movement that aims to establish a worldwide Islamic state by peaceful means. In banning the organization, the Kremlin argued that it is irrelevant whether it campaigns for a caliphate by armed or peaceful means; what matters is that its members don't recognize the existing authorities and openly speak out against them.

The security services have arrested a handful of Hizb ut-Tahrir members in Chelyabinsk and the neighboring region of Bashkortostan, which is predominantly Bashkir Muslim. They were not involved in any violence, but unconfirmed reports of a network of underground cells had created concern. A young journalist who covers the security services for an influential local online news outlet is downright alarmed. Despite the few arrests, she says, "extremists are popping up like mushrooms after a rain." She would like to see the government force all Muslims to observe their religion through one Kremlin-controlled authority. An Orthodox believer, she says, "I am against this excessive tolerance, that we need to respect other religions."

■

After three years of living under crippling investigation, Vilyard Yakupov is putting his life back together, though he remains under constant surveillance. Friends are regularly called in and asked what he is up to. The security services demanded Imam Istamgulov provide the names of the thirty or so people who continue to attend Saturday classes, threatening him with jail if he didn't comply. He thought about it and said, "I am seventy-five, and they can jail or kill me." He refused.

Yakupov has restored some old tractors and combines he bought, selling them for a profit. He makes excellent honey and is now investing in a herd of horses to produce kumiss, the fermented mare's milk that is popular with the local communities. So far he's had trouble getting access to local state-owned land, even though it is abandoned and lies fallow.

THIRTEEN

THE HUMAN RIGHTS
ACTIVISTS

On a frigid November day in 2012, inmates at a high-security prison in Chelyabinsk mounted an unprecedented peaceful protest against the constant beatings and torture sessions they claimed were being carried out by prison officials seeking pay-offs. There had been earlier, smaller protests in various detention centers, with dozens of prisoners cutting themselves to protest conditions, but the scale of this one, involving almost all the fifteen hundred inmates, was a first. This time, their strike was massive, strikingly nonviolent, and public. A commission had long documented widespread violations inside the region's prison system, but prosecutors and prison officials had repeatedly dismissed its complaints. The inmates at Prison No. 6 in the town of Kopeysk finally reached a breaking point, but they didn't break anything. They did no damage. They did not injure any guards. And this is what finally brought national attention.

It was visiting day. Family members had gathered outside, but their visits were suddenly canceled without explanation. Prisoners waiting inside broke away from their guards. Some reached the roof of a barracks. Others climbed a water tower. They stood out in the subzero temperatures for three days, displaying sheets painted with their demands: "People help," "Stop the torture," and "End the extortion." Relatives tossed cell phones over the brick and barbed-wire fences so that prisoners could describe to the world what was going on. The only violence occurred when special forces turned up. With no warning, they started beating family members standing by the gates. Images flooded the Internet. Journalists from across the country could not ignore what was going on, even if they wanted to. Nervous officials from Moscow arrived to open negotiations.

Nikolai Schur, a human rights activist and one of the few independent members of the government's prison commission, had long been documenting the widespread corruption in the Chelyabinsk prison system. At first glance, with his blunt-cut bangs and shaggy hair, he brings to mind Martin Luther, the sixteenth-century church reformer. Amid new Russian extravagance, he looks like an ascetic. He doesn't smoke and rarely drinks. He's been married to the same woman for more than forty years. He and Tatiana, who also secured a seat on the commission, are a powerful team.

Schur didn't nail his proclamations against prison abuse on any door. He did one better. He skillfully used detective work, the videotaped testimony of prisoners, the Internet, and intrepid journalists to make sure information got out and was not buried as it had been in the past. He emboldened prisoners and their families who had silently tolerated abuse and financial ruin.

He and Tatiana work together out of a tiny one-room office that is hard to find, given the glass-recycling operation in the yard below and the drunks bringing in their bottles. Up a crumbling stairway seemingly leading nowhere, they maintain a human rights organization. The first thing you see when you walk in is a portrait of Andrei Sakharov, the nuclear physicist turned human rights champion who defied Soviet power and died just as it was collapsing.

They get money wherever they can, from private Russian donors, from the Russian government's human rights commission, and still, most of all, from foreign sources such as George Soros and the U.S.-government-supported National Endowment for Democracy. By virtue of punctilious accounting, they have survived efforts by the tax police to shut them down. They have yet to be declared a "foreign agent"—a dangerous and pejorative appellation often attached to human rights organizations that receive funds from abroad for vaguely defined "political activity."

Now in his sixties, Schur is a mixture of many things. He's sardonic, sarcastic, pragmatic, and patient. He is angry, but he is not bitter. A highly skilled engineer who specialized in metrology, the science of measurement, he has a searing mind for detail. Tatiana is a chemist by training, though she is also a natural diplomat with disarming charm. The mother of three grown children and faced with constant challenges and threats, she looks remarkably youthful, and this without the benefit of Russia's new passion for face-lifts. Her eyes naturally sparkle. With rare lapses, she too remains enthusiastic.

The Schurs live in Snezhinsk, a research center comparable to Los Alamos. Like Ozersk, it is part of the country's archipelago of nuclear weapons cities, closed to all but residents and those with security passes. Once known only by its postal code, its post-Soviet name means "Snowy." Nikolai and Tatiana moved to postal code 70 back in 1984, where they became members of the Soviet scientific elite. Tatiana remembers how surprised she was to find meat in the shops in those years of shortages. Everyone got an apartment. When the Soviet Union collapsed, and with it Russia's economy, state employees often weren't paid. That included the nuclear scientists. Tatiana suggested that perhaps the nuclear researchers should think about diversifying; perhaps they should produce something the burgeoning consumer society wanted. "What," she recalls they said with horror, "you want us to make casserole dishes?" Yes, that was one possibility she had in mind because there were none. The discussion went nowhere. The government, initially with U.S. help, restored salaries, lest unhappy nuclear researchers sell their expertise to higher bidders such as renegade states or terrorist groups. Weapons work continues. There have been efforts to spin off new businesses, adopting nuclear technology for civilian uses like MRIs and medicines, but progress has been spotty.

Closed cities like Snezhinsk no longer have the allure they once had. The city remains under the control of Russia's Nuclear Ministry and the security services. The Schurs say workers are once again relatively well paid, though given the restrictions on who can enter and do business, it is no longer better supplied than other cities. Like Ozersk, the other closed city in the region, the most often-heard complaint is that it's boring. In 2013, a glamorous young student at one of Snezhinsk's science institutes made news when she wrote an open letter to President Vladimir Putin pleading with him to do something to make life more interesting for young people in the "forbidden" zones. Because of the restrictions on people and businesses, the young bemoan dull stores, dull entertainment, and the frustration of being unable to invite friends in from outside. Her letter sparked yet another debate over whether the closed cities should be opened. Given the subsequent spy-mania, and growing military confrontation with the West, that debate has disappeared.

The Schurs commute to Chelyabinsk to do their work but continue to live in Snezhinsk because if they sold their apartment, they wouldn't be able to find comparable space in the regional capital. One of their daughters lives with them. Her husband abandoned her after she gave birth to twins, one of whom has severe developmental problems. Most young people, however, try to get out. The city is aging. According to Tatiana, the one benefit is that given the overwhelming security in such a place, it is safe. You don't have to lock your car.

It was the city's pollution, the result of Soviet neglect, that initially propelled the Schurs' civic actions. When Mikhail Gorbachev began loosening the reins of power in the mid-1980s, the environment was the first "safe" problem that Russians could openly protest. On a balmy summer evening in 1988, I watched as activists held one of their first public meetings in a Moscow park, not far from the Kremlin. Hundreds gathered, with confused police standing on the sidelines. The assembled were stunned at their own audacity, wondering with each passing minute when the crackdown would start. The speakers were cautious, urging supporters to stick to issues of pollution, not politics, and the meeting went on unmolested. It was the beginning of the end.

This golden age of environmentalism spread across Russia as more and more information became available about once-hidden industrial and nuclear accidents. In the early 1990s, the Russian parliament passed a law demanding that factories and institutions responsible for pollution pay into an independent fund to clean it up. Nikolai Schur pays attention to details others don't see. He quickly seized the opportunity. He applied for and received permission to run the local fund in Snezhinsk.

He immediately established that only a small fraction of the money owed by some of the nation's biggest polluters was being collected. He forced them to pay up, and with that his troubles began. A senior city official who'd previously been head of police approached him, noting he was in control of a lot of money. He demanded a cut: "Bring me twenty thousand rubles tonight," he ordered. When Schur refused, this official accused him of using funds for personal gain. Nikolai Schur's file was growing.

In the meantime, Schur had set up an independent research lab, scoured the poverty-stricken country for hard-to-find equipment, and hired experts. In those heady times, before enthusiasm and bravery were largely snuffed out, local nuclear workers pointed out the most dangerous sites. Schur and his team launched their first investigations. They found dozens of "hot spots," many next to schools or playgrounds. In some cases, radiation levels were four thousand times those allowed.

He put together a film of his findings and took it to the local

TV station on a Friday night "when the bosses were out having a good time." Persuaded by Schur's careful documentation and the city's high cancer rate, the staff on duty agreed to run it. Residents who saw the broadcast immediately began to call the authorities. On Monday morning, agents from the FSB came to Schur's office. He realized then "my fate was sealed."

The nuclear weapons institute responsible for the worst radiation leaks immediately called Schur's reports a pack of lies. City residents then organized a meeting, inviting both him and representatives of the institute. The FSB repeatedly warned Schur not to go. The police and senior government officials also weighed in, warning him to stay away. "Naturally," he says, "I went." The head of safety for the institute then told the assembled, "There is nothing to be worried about." To reassure the crowd, he added, "After all, we are government officials." The residents were not reassured, and Schur suggested they all go together, with measuring equipment, to check out the sites in question. The head of the institute then turned to him, so all could hear, hissing, "I am sick of you. We will put you in prison." And they did.

Schur spent six months in jail, awaiting trial for alleged misuse of funds. Officials hoped his long detention would force him to give up and admit to some infraction. He was allowed no meetings with his wife and no letters. At the time, one of their daughters was on a U.S. government high school scholarship. In order to avoid upsetting her, Schur finally got the permission to write just to her. He composed twenty-seven letters at one sitting, concocting news of a humdrum existence, the passage of birthdays, and the changing seasons. They were passed on to his wife, who then posted them every week. According to Nikolai, his daughter Masha has yet to forgive him for this deception, protesting, "If I had only known, I would have organized such a campaign!"

As I have said, Schur is careful. He had kept excellent financial records. In the end, the authorities claimed he had stolen all of three dollars. For this, they gave both him and Tatiana suspended sentences of two to two and a half years. Those sentences guaranteed there would be limits on their future civic activities. Eager to demonstrate that the authorities had falsified evidence, and to ensure his ability to keep doing human rights work, Nikolai appealed. The prosecutor, confessing privately that he was under huge pressure to maintain the conviction, warned Schur that if he continued to maintain his innocence, it would be even worse. Schur withdrew his appeal. Nonetheless, the prosecutor went ahead and put in for a stricter sentence. At a subsequent trial, the judge asked Nikolai if he was happy with the sentence. "Of course I'm not," he said. "Then why don't you appeal?" the judge asked. Schur explained how he had been threatened. Using the limited powers he had, the judge tried to help. After long deliberation, he manipulated the system. He left the original sentence in place but imposed an amnesty so Nikolai and Tatiana would not suffer restrictions on their future work.

The environmental fund had since been shut down. Businesses no longer paid in, despite the law. But there were new opportunities. After his reelection in 1996, President Boris Yeltsin voiced support for human rights organizations. Schur, ever vigilant to political winds, quickly registered new NGOs with the local authorities that gave him legal status to pursue a range of civic activities. He applied for and received foreign grants, which were plentiful in those days. He and Tatiana began a local newspaper. They published the Universal Declaration of Human Rights, which a local editor had tried and failed to do. Though a seemingly mundane step, this was before the Internet, and Schur says it was "a bomb" for a closed nuclear weapons city.

The Schurs expanded their range of investigations. Environmental issues remained important to them. The most explosive concerned the sale of radioactive fish to schools, orphanages, hospitals, and old-age homes.

The good news was that public pressure had led the

government to rehabilitate some of the land that had been contaminated by decades of radioactive leaks. Fishing was banned in certain lakes deemed particularly dangerous, but harvesting eggs from the contaminated fish was permitted. The eggs were considered safe, and many of them were transferred to clean water, where they were incubated. The licenses for this business often went to relatives of top officials. But these well-connected businessmen weren't satisfied. For those looking for quick cash, the temptation to net and sell the poisonous fish, as well as incubate eggs, was just too great. They could not get a license to sell the fish on the open market, but through their connections they started supplying unsuspecting government institutions, like schools and orphanages.

Schur found out about this and wrote to the local representative of the newly elected president, Putin. The response was immediate: "There are no problems." Schur wrote again. This time his letter dripped with sarcasm. "I did not understand the role of the regional presidential representative, since this is not envisaged in the constitution, but now I understand it is to cover up the crimes of the authorities. Thank you for opening my eyes."

The presidential representative threatened Schur with prison, a threat he was getting all too used to. This time it was for insulting the government. Schur asked, "For what?" He suggested the two of them test the fish in question.

Schur invited journalists and others to witness his inquiry. Police blocked the roads to keep them away and locked reporters in their hotels so they could not get out, but some escaped. A senior official in attendance threatened him again.

This time the authorities failed; the media coverage was too overwhelming. But this was the last gasp of a free press. Vladimir Putin would muzzle most national television coverage in the future. His appointed governor in Chelyabinsk would take care of local press. The heydays of the 1990s were over.

Because Nikolai and Tatiana still live in a closed city, their friends, whether Russian or foreign, cannot visit them there. But they also own a run-down village house outside the exclusion zone that they purchased in the middle of the first decade of the twenty-first century. Before buying the house, Nikolai first tested the ground and local water for danger. He found a safe area, albeit one surrounded by toxicity. This seems fitting, given that he remains a rare voice of conscience in a corrupted world.

The village house is a forty-minute drive from their apartment in Snezhinsk and three hours from Chelyabinsk, where they maintain their office. They picked me up one morning in the regional capital. As we headed out of Chelyabinsk, we stopped along the way to stock up at the *rinok*, a central market brimming with stalls. Nikolai can seem stern when focusing on work, and with good reason, but if you get him in the market, he is like a kid. He has few indulgences, but good Russian food is one of them. Before the Western sanctions of 2014, well-stocked supermarkets, packed with a huge range of imported, prepared, and processed foods, were everywhere. But the *rinok* remains a real farmers' market. While such markets spread in America, they've become rarer now in Russia, as increasingly urban Russians become entranced by convenience. The "central" market is now a bit out of the way, and prices are a bit higher, but the atmosphere remains seductive, and the produce delicious: there's a huge selection of homemade sausages and smoked meats, local cheeses, fresh bread, plump fruits and vegetables from local farms and those in the southern former Soviet republics, a homemade beer known as kvass, and the delight of chatter and gossip. Everyone in the market knows Nikolai, and in his own naughty way he delights in introducing me to all the stall keepers. Despite growing anti-Americanism, they are not put off by a foreigner and respond with curiosity and generosity, offering free tastes of everything. Within minutes, I have eaten a sumptuous meal.

Laden with supplies, we head out to the family dacha, a somewhat restored wreck of a house in a remote decaying village on the shore of one of Chelyabinsk's many lakes. On the fence out-side, one of his daughters has painted a rendition of Nikolai fishing from a yellow submarine, an inside joke about his "inner hippie." Everyone down to a cluster of grandchildren gathers here as often as they can to ski, snuggle, skate, and, best of all, sled down a homemade slide onto the frozen lake. When the weather warms, there's swimming, fishing, mushroom collecting, and ferocious gardening.

The house is frigid. The original log cabin is now the site of a kitchen and bedroom. The family has gradually turned adja-cent animal sheds into comfortable, if modest, additional living spaces, linking them all to form an inner courtyard. Cinder blocks used to cover the decaying sheds are painted in fanciful colors, dotted with old CDs that glisten in the sun and glimmer in the moonlight. Artifacts from the Soviet past are tacked up along the roofline to create a family "museum"; there are curious tools and long-abandoned kitchen implements, an abacus (they were once used in every shop), and a shortwave radio receiver, reminis-cent of days when the only "real" news came crackling and jammed from overseas. Down a steep stairwell, there is a cellar where the family stores produce from their summer garden—mounds of carrots, potatoes, and onions. There is also a freezer, packed with frozen berries collected during the warmer months. Nikolai retrieves fish he caught and starts a fire outside to smoke them.

It's the first real snow of a surprisingly late season, and bun-dled up against the crisp cold, we walk through the village, a cluster of one-story wooden houses with few signs of renovations or new construction. The church remains a ruin. The local state farm has long been closed. The secondary school has been shut-tered. As is the case with most Russian villages, the young have long decamped in search of jobs and entertainment elsewhere. The crunch of our boots is the only sound. Breaking the silence, I ask Nikolai why he has taken on the government. "Why you?" I ask.

One of his grandfathers was a tsarist officer and a village religious leader who was sent to the camps. The other was a committed Bolshevik who was eventually devoured by the revolution he supported. He was shot in 1937. Schur's father was captured by the Germans in World War II. Following his liberation and repatriation by U.S. forces, a sin in Stalin's books, he was imprisoned on his return home. He was a metalworker by trade, and that, according to Schur, is what saved him. The Soviet Union was desperate for skilled laborers, given the toll the war and Stalin's purges had taken. Schur's father was eventually sent to work in a Chelyabinsk factory. Though he could live with his family, his movements were restricted until 1957. Unlike many families where Stalin's persecutions were never discussed, and usually hidden, Schur says his family was open about the past. "My father," he says, "was an enemy of the unjust Soviet system."

By the time we return home, the fish is smoked, and the wood-burning stoves have warmed the house. As we strip off our layers of clothing, Nikolai's cell phone is ringing. It is the criminal investigator pursuing the case against the head of Prison No. 6, where prisoners had protested brutal corruption. He says the case is going forward. Clearly he wants Nikolai to spread the word to journalists so it will be that much more difficult for the prosecutor's office to reverse the decision.

For Nikolai and Tatiana, this is the culmination of three years of work. There is the clink of teacups, but Nikolai warns they have yet to see what the exact charges are. Nor is it clear how the prosecutor's office will respond despite the overwhelming evidence of official abuse.

In 2008, the Russian government created regional commissions to monitor conditions in prisons. Almost all the members were selected by President Putin or his appointees. Though the commissions were stacked with those who would not question the status quo, a limited number of slots were given to human rights organizations.

As usual, Nikolai paid close attention to these new opportunities. Despite resistance, he and Tatiana fulfilled all the requirements, got backing from human rights activists in Moscow, and were named to the Chelyabinsk commission. As such, they have the right to visit any detention center when they wish. While many commission members have done nothing, a small group led by the Schurs has worked hard to document violations.

One of the first cases they came across was that of a man who had killed six people. He had once worked in a military factory, but when salaries stopped in the 1990s, he went out on his own to fix cars. Thugs turned up demanding *roof*, the word in Russian for protection money. He refused to pay. To persuade him, they took him to a house out of town where they put a gun to his head and then ushered him into a room where his friend's wife was being raped. His wife had also been kidnapped, and she was apparently next. This man went home, got a gun, returned, and killed the thugs. He was convicted and sentenced to fifteen years.

He was an ideal prisoner and came up for early release. But there was an unofficial price—ten thousand dollars. He paid the judge, but the head of the prison was apparently unhappy that he had not received his cut. He blocked the deal.

That was one of the first inklings the Schurs got about the corruption inside Russian prisons. In the course of dozens of visits since then, they found a pattern of shakedowns, beatings, torture, and in some cases murder by prison staff. Prisoners were regularly forced to come up with so-called voluntary humanitarian help, allegedly to improve prison conditions. This was a euphemism for bribes, which ranged from monthly payments of a hundred dollars to tens of thousands of dollars or the equivalent in goods. There were "fees" to use the phone, see one's family, get medical care, or be considered for parole. Punishment for refusing to pay up was solitary confinement for weeks or months, beatings, and torture.

Until Nikolai and Tatiana started visiting, there was no way for prisoners to complain. Their letters were censored or destroyed. What complaints did reach the prosecutor's office were ignored. And those who dared to complain were punished further.

It wasn't easy to get prisoners to talk about conditions. They were frightened of what would happen when the Schurs left. Nikolai and Tatiana learned that they had to visit regularly to limit any repercussions. With the prisoners' permission, they often videotaped their interviews and put the material on the Internet. One prisoner who testified on tape said, "If I subsequently change my testimony, shown in this video, it means I have given in to the torture of guards."

There were bad living conditions—absence of windows and natural light, absence of artificial light, and lack of sheets and blankets. Access to qualified medical treatment was difficult. Several prisons boasted good libraries and sports facilities, but prisoners weren't allowed to use them on a regular basis. They were largely to impress visiting officials and commissions. TV news was censored, a violation of the law. There were damp rooms, leaking ceilings, fungus growing on the walls, bad ventilation, and rats, lots of them.

When work was available, prisoners were forced to work far more than the legal eight hours a day to fulfill quotas, which were not specified, and they often received the equivalent of two dollars a month, far less than the legal minimum. Frequently, the work was dangerous. At one prison, inmates were required to clean bloody syringes and drips without protective gloves.

But all this was nothing compared with the secret cells, concealed in basements or camouflaged by fake bookshelves, which the Schurs eventually located in just about every prison. Inmates likely to complain were often hidden there during the Schurs' visits. And it was here that prisoners suffered "the net." Those who misbehaved, refused to work, or didn't come up with "humanitarian assistance" were taped to the mesh cell wall and hung for hours, sometimes days, while guards or co-opted inmates beat them and administered electric shocks. Pencils were inserted between their fingers and twisted. Unbearably loud music was constantly played to mask the screams and enhance the punishment.

Though competition is stiff, the award for worst prison in Chelyabinsk has to go to No. 6—the prison where the prisoners finally went on strike. What the Schurs had long documented was subsequently confirmed by a presidential commission from Moscow. It received 621 complaints in sealed envelopes, detailing the abuses, including the amounts inmates and their families had been forced to pay and to whom.

Thanks to the Schurs, the worst beatings, torture, and shakedowns have reportedly stopped, but Nikolai says, "We are not so naive to think that this improved situation will necessarily continue." Prison authorities still demand money, but the amounts are much less. For now, there is an agreement between the prisoners and the staff. If inmates pay up the reduced amounts, keep mum, and stop complaining, there will be no more beatings. As Schur puts it, "If in the past they gave them no bread, now they give them a crust."

Schur's advice to families is "Don't pay. Don't believe that your loved one's life will be easier. Sometimes it works, but there will come a time when you will run out of money, you will be in debt, you will have lost your apartment, and they will start to beat him again. It's your choice, and don't forget that if you pay, you are implicated."

As the investigation into Prison No. 6 dragged on, Schur's fears proved to be well-founded. Many of those who had provided testimony were threatened. Some were still in custody, controlled by the very people they were accusing. Key witnesses withdrew their stories, though in some cases they had earlier said that if they did so, it would only be due to intolerable pressure. That was not taken into consideration, nor were the threats investigated.

The head of the prison, Major Denis Mekhanov, was eventually given a three-year suspended sentence, despite threats to witnesses and the well-documented history of systematic extortion, threats, beatings, and torture. Schur calls this an insult to the victims and yet another disgrace for the justice system. He continues to monitor prison conditions.

New complaints suggest that prison authorities are offering inmates with military experience a chance for early release if they go as "volunteers" to fight in Ukraine. Should they refuse the offer, sources indicate they will lose any chance of parole and be further punished.

FOURTEEN

THE FORENSIC EXPERT

On a brisk autumn day, a friend takes me to the outskirts of Chelyabinsk, past the gloomy factories and past a glimmering reservoir to a stretch of woods where land prices have skyrocketed and high-end developments are planned. But that's not why we are here.

We nearly miss the turnoff, a sharp right onto a dirt track that meanders through a birch forest. The afternoon sun flickers off the black-and-white bark. There aren't any signs, but we finally reach our destination, a glade dotted with crude crosses. Some are made of rough-hewn wood, others of simple iron. Bouquets of garish fake flowers are propped at the base of some of the crosses or left to hang, gently swishing in the breeze. Most crosses have a terse but telling handwritten sign: "Andrei Sinschin, shot in 1938" . . . "Alexander Antiufeev, Pastor of Church, shot 1938" . . . "Yusif Khorvat 1896–1938." There is one site dedicated to twenty-three Russian Orthodox priests executed in 1937. In the center of the clearing is a large rock placed in 1989 with the words "Here will be a permanent memorial to the victims of Stalin's illegal repressions."

All these years later, there is still no permanent memorial. Stalin's legacy is no longer repudiated by the Kremlin, and the

Russian Orthodox Church is now reluctant to dwell on his crimes, focusing instead on what they call his positive achievements.

In 1989, when the Soviet Union's secrets were finally emerging from the shadows, local members of the newly formed organization Memorial got tips about a possible mass grave. Founded under the auspices of Andrei Sakharov, Memorial was dedicated to documenting the fate of the millions who had been imprisoned, exiled, or killed by Joseph Stalin and his henchmen. It was also committed to defending rights in the new Russia.

In the late 1930s, nearby villagers had heard volleys of gunshots night after night and suspected the Soviet security services were using a long-abandoned gold mine as a killing ground, but no one investigated. No one dared even talk about it until the late 1980s, when, under Mikhail Gorbachev, the Soviet Union's history of repression could at last be openly discussed. As Memorial's local volunteers began to scrape around the old mine shafts, they found scattered bones, and then they uncovered complete skeletons.

Alexander Vlasov, the region's deputy forensic pathologist, agreed to help them. He little suspected how much he was risking his career. After all, these were the glasnost years. Journals and newspapers were full of once-banned articles about the past. Families were finally revealing long-hidden secrets about relatives who disappeared into Stalin's gulag. The KGB was opening archives so people could read the files of loved ones. In many cases, those files revealed that many innocent prisoners believed right until the end that Stalin or honest courts would intervene to stop what they took to be the "renegade" actions of officials.

In Chelyabinsk, snow had not yet fallen, and Memorial's volunteers began to excavate the entrances to three or four mine shafts—each an area thirty feet in diameter. They were full of bodies, packed one on top of the other. Buttons and rubber soles were all that remained of the clothing. Alexander Vlasov showed the volunteers how to properly remove the skeletons and store them in paper. There were no body bags in those days.

Moving slowly, the volunteers retrieved a total of four hundred bodies. They had dug barely a foot. Vlasov estimates the mine shafts, perhaps a total of ten in all, were each three hundred feet deep. By his calculation, that would mean there were possibly tens of thousands of bodies dumped there. "Too many," he said, shaking his head. "Too many," he repeated again and again.

Vlasov took the excavated remains to his lab for analysis, where his examination indicated the victims had been shot in the head or in some cases stabbed with bayonets. There were more shafts and tunnels to be explored. This was just the beginning.

According to Vlasov, "We didn't hide what we were doing, and initially the authorities did not interfere." But a British film crew came to document their work. When word got out that there were skeletons of children and that some of the victims had been killed in the late 1940s, long after the worst of the repressions were supposed to have ended, the KGB suddenly appeared. After a few months, Memorial was forbidden to do any further excavations. Vlasov was told to stop his work. The remains he was examining in his lab disappeared one night. The grave site was inexplicably filled in and is now just a series of low grassy humps, its secrets still buried.

To this day, it's not clear who was actually shot and dumped in this spot. There may well be records somewhere—the Soviet authorities were creepily punctilious at documenting their crimes—but the actual identities of the victims have yet to be revealed. The site has become a symbolic cemetery for all those who perished in Chelyabinsk, and almost every family has some close relative who disappeared.

Vlasov paid for his "unofficial" work. Until the late 1980s, he had worked for the state, often with the security forces, but his attitude to them, and theirs to him, changed after he assisted

Memorial and spoke out about his findings. He wasn't fired, but as punishment he was forbidden to defend his doctoral thesis, a study on how to determine the time of death.

With the economic crisis of the early 1990s, he, like many in Chelyabinsk, could not survive on his official salary even if it was paid. His wife, Irina, a pediatrician, was making the equivalent of ten dollars a month. Given the official displeasure with his activities, and to support his family, Vlasov decided to go out on his own. Given his training as a forensic pathologist, what better new career than as a funeral director?

Death has a peculiar hold on Russians, perhaps because they die relatively young, perhaps because life for most has not been easy and the Orthodox faith promises better in the beyond. In the composer Tchaikovsky's house, now a remarkable museum an hour's drive from Moscow, there is a death corner with photographs of close friends lying rigid in their open coffins.

For centuries, many dead Russians were buried with more luxury and respect than they enjoyed in life. The Russian Orthodox Church's traditions survived even in Soviet times. Funerals involved open coffins and elaborate burials. Most Russian graves are marked by a simple cross or headstone, with a photograph of the deceased embedded under glass. But gravestones can also be fanciful memorials to lives once lived, and Russian cemeteries are among the most interesting places to visit. A giant propeller adorns a burial place for a pilot; a bust depicts a Soviet military commander giving orders, telephone clasped to his ear. In Moscow, the monument to Stalin's second wife, who may have committed suicide, is a haunting sculpture of a beautiful, tortured woman. Even at the height of antireligious propaganda, she was buried in hallowed ground, the cemetery of a former convent. The Soviet leader Nikita Khrushchev was also buried there. His bust was rendered by an artist he once excoriated as depraved in telling shades of black-and-white stone, a less-than-subtle commentary on Khrushchev's complex character and legacy. Cultural and scientific figures are honored with carvings evoking their achievements. Prominent officials are typically memorialized with elaborate marble and black granite headstones bearing etched portraits.

After nine days, and again after forty, Orthodox rites call for further feasts to mark the passage of the soul from the body to another world. On birthdays and the anniversaries of deaths, tradition dictates a visit to the graves of relatives or other beloved figures like writers. I recall how dozens gathered to commemorate the 1960 death of Boris Pasternak, the author of *Doctor Zhivago*. Decades after his demise, his fans still braved sleet and frigid winds to recite by heart excerpts from his work. His headstone was invisible, covered by mounds of flowers.

On Easter, it is common for families to remember the dead and feed their souls in graveside picnics with ritual bread and pieces of decorated eggs and flowers. Crumbs are often scattered on the grave to feed the birds, symbols of the soul that rose up from the ground. As one Russian friend put it, cemeteries for us are "a sacred site of social interchange between the living and the dead."

Because everyone worked for the state, Soviet funerals had been supported by government employers. But when hard times hit in the late 1980s and early 1990s, factories no longer had the money. Worried about their own death throes, they dispensed with burial services. As living became more difficult, death became ignominious. The bereaved were left to build the coffins and dig the graves themselves. "It was unacceptable and demeaning," says Vlasov's wife, Irina.

In his new endeavor as a funeral director, Vlasov initially had no competition. Finding the necessary materials, however, proved more complicated. Hardware stores were still only a dream in post-Soviet Chelyabinsk. It took creativity to find nails and boards. Vlasov describes taking apart fences to make the first coffins.

Vlasov's customer base was clear: there were ordinary people seeking dignity in death, as well as a whole new class of people who had plenty of money and who wanted funerals, cost no object, with imported silk-lined ebony coffins. Vlasov started to travel to Italy and Cyprus to satisfy the tastes of the new rich, most of them criminals; he would return with high-priced coffins in Aeroflot's hold. There's a classic "mafia" burial plot a few hours' drive from Chelyabinsk, filled with notorious members of the local mob who thrived in the 1990s. The dead are all captured in a variety of lifelike poses, their leather jackets and jeans immortalized in eight-foot-tall expensive black marble slabs erected in a row. These were among Vlasov's best customers.

The new funeral business, catering to the modest and the absurd, expanded to include parlors across the city. It was extremely profitable. The Vlasov family moved into one of the first chic gated buildings to sprout in the center of town, a building where the intercom works, a desk attendant pays attention, and the sleek entryway and elevator are free from crude graffiti, garbage, and cigarette butts.

The spacious apartment is everything their Soviet slum was not. It has high ceilings and big rooms. A designer had a hand in it. Their former tacky Soviet furniture has been replaced by expensive imported leather. The kitchen remains the center of life, but it is now an open-plan kitchen with a central island, all the most modern appliances, and a large table ready to serve guests. A balcony conveniently leads to the next-door apartment, where Vlasov's son and his family live well off the largesse of Papa. A much-beloved grandson races in wearing a Disney World T-shirt.

Irina is made-up and well coiffed; her expertly dyed blond hair is cut in a sophisticated bob. Returning from errands, she quickly exchanges her mink coat, black designer trousers, sweater, and Chanel necklace for a simple housedress. Now retired at sixty plus, this former pediatrician is juggling disparate roles. She is at once a glamorous aging woman, a devoted grandmother, a frustrated former doctor, and a vigilant wife to a difficult husband. The seeming sweetness of wealth has turned her bitter. The luxury they live in has come with intimidation, death threats, and jail time as part of the bill. As Alexander Vlasov joins us in the kitchen, Irina deftly prepares meat pies, sliced salmon, and a variety of delicious Russian salads, constantly refilling glasses with champagne while not missing a word, though she knows the story all too well and it's a long one.

As his funeral business prospered, Vlasov came under pressure to pay off city officials. He resisted, convinced perhaps he had protection from other quarters. At the same time, he watched acquaintances pay for their stubbornness with their lives. Arkady Fisher, a friend, was shot point-blank in his factory office during a battle over the privatization of state firms. Vlasov says everyone knew who the gunman was, and he was sure he could solve the case, given his forensic skills, but officials "not surprisingly weren't interested." The 1990s saw a dramatic increase in contract murders as competing forces fought over new business opportunities and access to property and land.

One morning, as Vlasov pulled out onto the street, he heard something fall off the car. He stopped to see what had gone *ker-thunk*. On the pavement was an unexploded grenade, which had fortunately been badly taped to the underbelly of his vehicle. Then there was the day the police arrived to search his office. They found two thousand dollars in his safe—a not unusual event, it should be noted, because no one then had any faith in banks. They claimed the money was fake and didn't return it. In 2001, the prosecutor accused Vlasov of giving bribes "to unknown people, in unknown amounts, in unknown places." Vlasov says he was arrested because he refused to pay off high-level officials.

Vlasov spent two months in prison awaiting trial. Taking another sip of champagne, he tries to laugh it all off, but it was far from clear what his fate would be, and his wife finds recalling that time makes her fearful to this day. Gesturing to the dining area, to show how small the space was, he tells how he was initially put in a holding cell with seventy-five other prisoners. There was barely enough room to stand, let alone sleep. He couldn't take it, and given his long acquaintance with the prison authorities he managed to move to slightly more commodious accommodations—from a room with only thirty-five to a cell where everyone still had to sleep by turn. He says prison officers and prisoners knew why he was being punished and were somewhat sympathetic. He did not have to wear handcuffs. He was brought a cake on his fiftieth birthday, a day he has not forgotten. He became an adviser to other prisoners on the merits, or lack thereof, of their cases. Every evening he held consultations. When he was finally released, the head of the prison noted how smart the prisoners had become under his tutelage.

Vlasov chuckles again recalling those days, perhaps because compared with what was to come, they were child's play. He was given a two-year suspended sentence. That's the equivalent of an acquittal in a system where an honest judge dare not directly challenge the prosecution but in some cases will find a way to compromise. At this point in our conversation, Irina, flipping dumplings, breaks into a snippet from *Cabaret*, singing "Money money."

Vlasov is a gambler by nature, and a very good one by all accounts, especially at poker. "I like beating the house," he says with a twinkle, his rotting, nicotine-stained teeth breaking into a disarming grin. Vlasov is nothing if not charming, not to mention wily.

In the 1990s, gambling took off across Russia, with the flashy lights of casinos dotting every city. Chelyabinsk was no exception, and Vlasov was often to be found—much to his wife's despair—in the more elegant casinos. On one occasion, he proudly says, he won four cars that he traded in for cash. He wrote a book about poker, and he was so good the casinos wanted to keep him out. In 2008, the government ordered the country's vast numbers of casinos shut down, with plans to establish a few remote places where they would be permitted and monitored—Russia's version of Las Vegas. Today, there are plenty of underground dens for inveterate gamblers. Vlasov, who apparently keeps in touch with this underworld, estimates there are 178 illegal gambling joints in town. But he says the charm has gone. During one of my many walks around Chelyabinsk, I happened to enter a couple of un-marked doors, only to find dimly lit barrooms chock-full of one-armed bandits right in the center of the city with police patrolling just a few feet away. "How can this be?" I asked Vlasov. His an-swer: "Law enforcement officials control them and the police know it, so they won't touch them. They know their boundaries."

When he was released from prison, Vlasov dared to continue his funeral business, though on a more modest scale. He incor-rectly estimated the odds. Demands for payoffs dramatically increased after the appointment of a new mayor in 2005. Ac-cording to Vlasov, officials approached him with "requests" he pay a monthly fee of 100,000 rubles to continue his business. The next month the sum went up to 200,000 rubles. Then the price was raised again. He paid up, but by the fourth month the "right" to do business had reached a monthly fee of $16,000. It was too much, and Vlasov refused.

In 2008, his deputy was gunned down as he left their down-town office. A policeman witnessed the shooting and called for backup as the killer ran away. The killer was apprehended in a nearby park as he pulled off his mask and tried to throw away his weapon. He claimed a high-level official had paid him for the hit. The gunman was convicted but there were no investigations into his allegations. Further investigations and charges came to an abrupt end, allegedly for lack of evidence.

A message reached Vlasov: "You are next." He closed down his business but not without paying another "fee." He says a high-level official claimed he owed $400,000 on his headquarters in the center of town. Vlasov called in experts to prove the documents were falsified, but, he says, "as usual the court caved." He has protected many of the family assets by putting them in his wife's name, but he personally remains in debt and estimates it will take twenty years to pay it off. Until then, he is banned from traveling abroad. This rankles. On his desk is a real estate flyer for his former building, now up for sale for a cool $1.3 million.

The funeral business continues to be a windfall for local officials. Vlasov says his successors have to regularly pay bribes of $100,000 to stay in operation, though the officials thoughtfully don't also demand they pay taxes. The federal government says it wants to take over the burial business in order to clean it up, but Vlasov scoffs at its promises to bring order. With so much money to be pocketed, he calls it yet another "imitation fight against corruption."

Alexander Vlasov is now in his early sixties. He is too thin, he chain-smokes and drinks way too much brut, but he remains a dapper dresser, and his mind is as sharp as ever. He is a driven individual and a contrarian and has never lost his passion for science. Along the way, he set up a forensic institute. Initially a side business, meant to stimulate his intelligence if not his bank account, it is now his main endeavor, and he is one of the few independent forensic experts in the country.

At first, the institute didn't look promising. Defense lawyers were his first clients, and they had trouble introducing independent expertise in court. One judge who dared to support Vlasov's conclusions in 2000 was summarily fired.

Vlasov says judges are easily manipulated because they are appointed and can be fired with no stated reason. Chief judges are political appointees with historically close ties to the security services. They and the prosecution put constant pressure on other judges. Gesturing to the phone, Vlasov describes "telephone justice," whereby judges are told in advance how to resolve a case.

"Judges have traditionally gone through the pretense of asking questions as if they are checking material, but the decision has long been made. If a judge goes against that decision and acquits, and that acquittal is subsequently reversed by a more compliant higher court, the judge could face disciplinary charges and risk his career." This has resulted in a kind of self-censorship.

The prosecutor remains powerful and the justice system capricious, incompetent, and corrupt. Yet Vlasov has recently seen some judges get tougher with prosecutors and investigators, rejecting spurious evidence, at least in cases that are not politically sensitive. Vlasov attributes some of this growing "bravery" to the plummeting level of police work, which even cowed judges are hard-pressed to ignore. Because talented forensic experts are unwilling to work for the pittance the government pays, both the government and private clients increasingly turn to him to look into everything from building scams and forged documents to fires and murders.

An effort to get one of the more honest judges to speak to me failed. After making a couple of calls, Vlasov shook his head. "I thought he would go for it, but he is too scared." As if to emphasize the surreal nature of justice, a call interrupts us. It comes from a government official who works for the very man who once threatened Vlasov's life and might well have ordered his deputy's killing. They need his help on a case. Vlasov smiles at the absurdity of the situation: "They know I know what they did, and they know I don't like them, but today they need me."

For all his growing business, Vlasov still faces admonitions to the effect that "you can investigate this but not that." When guards in one of Chelyabinsk's prisons allegedly beat up and killed four prisoners, the prisoners' families hired Vlasov to investigate and examine the corpses. Security forces surrounded the morgue, denying Vlasov and the relatives access. Vlasov says, "The authorities then came to me and said, 'Don't put your nose in this, or it will be very bad for you.'"

In another case, a prisoner was alleged to have hanged himself. This time the family managed to obtain the body. Pretending that they were readying it for burial, they took it instead to Vlasov, who found massive evidence of beating. The government's forensic specialist had found none. Vlasov documented his findings with photographs, but he says government specialists, under pressure from above, refused to acknowledge the blatant evidence and the case was closed.

He travels the country, with more and more regions turning to him for help. The prosecutor from neighboring Orenburg approached him to assist in a military fraud case. Under a new law, the Defense Ministry was to provide headstones for servicemen who took part in conflicts—all the wars from World War II through Afghanistan and Chechnya. The Orenburg military headquarters commissioned a local funeral business to do the work. Together they put in receipts for 200 graves at the cost of $1,000 apiece. As proof, they provided photographs of the headstones, which were strikingly similar. The local prosecutor, suspecting something fishy and speculating that both military commanders and the funeral business might be in on a scam, turned to Vlasov for an independent evaluation. Vlasov was able to show that in fact only one headstone was ever made: it was repeatedly photoshopped with the names of 199 people who had no living relatives able to complain about the absence of any actual gravestone. "That's roughly $199,000 for sitting on a computer and doing a little fancy finger work," he chortles. Top officials ultimately rejected his evidence. It's an old Russian story in a new guise. The classic novel *Dead Souls* by Nikolai Gogol told a similar tale of making money from ghosts.

In Vlasov's office, packages of Parliament cigarettes clutter his desk, with a cabinet full of champagne and Hennessy within easy reach. On top of the cabinet stands a statue of Don Quixote. Over his head, there is a large wooden crucifix, which can only be a bitter joke. A confirmed atheist, Vlasov scoffs at man's desire to rely on a mysterious God or a government that seeks endorsement from the Orthodox Church. "It's the easy way out, and it's a great way for a government to have power, playing on this unquestioning belief and the utter passivity of the majority."

At our last meeting, he was resigned. He said most Russians are delighted to see Putin flexing his political and military muscle. After so many years of searching for a way to unite people, Putin has finally succeeded by creating foreign enemies. The next step is to reinforce the police state. Vlasov doesn't think anyone he knows will protest, whatever their views; he says they are older, are too Russian to survive outside the country, and have too much wealth at stake to risk it. "One step right and one step left and we'll lose it all."

As a sign of what's to come, he shows me a letter he recently received from the government. It demanded details about all his employees, including their racial makeup, religious and political views, intimate family history, and sexual orientation.

He refused and has been fined.

Vlasov says he was one of the first to be targeted under a long-existing but dormant law. He tells friends, and they don't believe him. They say just fill in the answers and lie. But Vlasov anticipates that it will be harder to finesse such requests in the future. Every enterprise may have to hire someone to address such questions. Though ostensibly on company payroll, such a person would ultimately be responsible to the security services.

FIFTEEN

FREEDOM OF SPEECH

You wouldn't notice Irina Gundareva at first glance, and that would be a mistake. She's somewhere in her early fifties, and far from flashy, with blunt-cut reddish hair and straight bangs. But beneath this modest exterior, she is fierce. Considered among the best journalists in Chelyabinsk, she regularly fought and won cases brought against her for libel and defamation, even in the region's corrupt courts. She has also confronted more sinister threats from officials and others she had displeased with her investigations.

She wrote a series of articles about connections between criminals and the city administration, focusing on illegal property transactions. Her garage, which was located in a disputed piece of real estate, coincidentally burned down. The fire department found evidence of plastic bottles with gasoline and declared it arson. The police refused to pursue the case.

She also tracked the suspicious theft of $150,000 from a Chelyabinsk businesswoman. Police had searched the woman's office—illegally, as it turned out—because of alleged tax violations. On their orders, she opened and emptied her safe, which contained two packages of cash she planned to use to buy an apartment. The police demanded she pay the equivalent of $20,000 in alleged back taxes on the spot. She wisely refused, and it was later established she owed nothing. As the police watched, she put the money back in the safe, locked it, and put away the key. Two days later, her office was broken into, the safe opened with the key, and the money taken. The police quickly closed the investigation, telling her to "forget it." When she wouldn't, they suggested she had stolen the money herself. They made a mistake if they thought she was a pushover. The businesswoman pursued her own investigation because the only people who knew there had been money in the safe were the officers, whose conduct had been questionable from the start. The more she followed up, the greater the questions and the greater the pushback, including veiled threats from authorities. The police refused to take lie detector tests. All documents surrounding the investigation mysteriously disappeared. Her investigation into the personal finances of the officer who had initially conducted the search of her office revealed he had suddenly come into money, buying a new apartment and car. His salary could not possibly cover any of this, and there was no family money to explain his purchases. His father was a poor pensioner, and his mother a cleaning lady.

When Irina followed up on all this and published an article, her son, a taxi driver, began to be harassed by police. They allegedly found marijuana in his car. His blood test, taken when his car was stopped, showed no signs of drugs. He was charged with drug possession. Knowing her son, Irina was sure he had been set up. Her boss at the newspaper refused to support her. Instead, the Moscow-based Glasnost Defense Foundation, which defends journalists, came to her aid, providing lawyers. Given her outstanding reputation, Glasnost would be able to make an international scandal, sometimes but not always effective. The case against her son was eventually dropped, but Irina had had it with her newspaper, which increasingly spiked her stories about corruption and human rights violations.

Irina has gone out on her own and opened a Web site where she can aggregate material and cover what the mainstream press won't touch. She continues to investigate local malfeasance and was one of the few local reporters to cover the opposition leader Alexei Navalny's trial and the subsequent protests, small as they were, in Chelyabinsk. If you had relied on local commercial news sites, you would have been hard-pressed to find information about the murder of the opposition leader Boris Nemtsov and the subsequent march by tens of thousands in Moscow. It was left to people like Irina.

She gets donations, but she does not have a huge readership, certainly not the three thousand unique daily readers that would require her to register with the authorities. But she is regularly reposted, and has yet another blog on LiveJournal, an influential Web site. She can fly below the radar, but she still worries about being set up again. Not long ago, another local journalist-activist was arrested while investigating environmental issues in a distant forest. He was allegedly found with "dangerous" weapons and a grenade. As it turned out, the planted weapons were out-of-date hunting rifles and the grenade merely a fake used for training. The police bungled their setup, and amazingly the judge called them on it, but it was a near miss.

As we talk, her phone rings. It's a businessman she has recently written about. Corrupt officials tried to illegally take over his business. He ultimately won in arbitration court. He calls to tell her he would not have succeeded without her diligent reporting. For a brief moment, she takes comfort in what she does. But later another call comes in, warning that her sources are known and "will be made unhappy."

Currently, her biggest concern is Ukraine and what she can write about it. She is appalled at the official media's one-sided, usually hysterical coverage. She says watching TV would compel anyone to take up arms and fight. When she has tried to post alternative views and correctives to the blatant lies of official outlets, she has been threatened by "volunteers" returning from

Ukraine, who claim to know her address and the names of her relatives.

She also continues to pursue official corruption. In a town on the outskirts of Chelyabinsk, residents and small businesses have long appealed to President Putin to stop what they alleged are the mayor's illegal land grabs and shakedowns. But as a Putin supporter, with close ties to the regional government and plenty of *kompromat* in his possession, he has been untouchable. Eventually, even some local elected officials, members of Putin's party, joined the protests. They invited Irina to a public hearing. Her presence as an accredited journalist was supported by law. Nonetheless, she was wrestled to the ground and physically ejected by the mayor's private security service. Those who invited her did nothing when push came to more than shove. She plans to go to court yet again.

"Why do you take these risks?" I ask her, my eternal question to those who challenge the system. Her simple answer: "Someone has to." She then explained that her grandfather died in Stalin's camps in 1936 for, as she puts it, "telling the truth." As in so many families, this was a long-kept secret. Her mother was desperate to hide the fact she was the daughter of "an enemy of the people." Irina only learned of his fate in the 1980s. Her grandfather is now her inspiration. She repeats an idea I hear so often, that Russia lost its best and brightest in the wars and purges: "I begin to think we are genetically flawed when I see how we so easily fall into a slave mentality." She would like to write more about the growing defense budget and its effects on other government programs. She has gathered material on Chelyabinsk units that have secretly been sent to Ukraine, but new, increasingly punitive laws against "extremism" hang over her. She grows weary of taking risks with less and less support from those around her. She thinks about leaving the country.

Russian journalists have often been murdered or severely

injured for writing investigative articles. In a country that boasts a high rate of successful investigations, such cases are seldom solved. The new laws, providing huge financial penalties for defamation or jail time for alleged "extremism," make murder unnecessary, and thus reduce the risk of drawing unwanted criticism from abroad. The authorities have become much more sophisticated at using money, economic weapons, vaguely worded laws, and often compliant courts against both reporters and their bosses.

■

Irina shrugs when I ask about the new generation of journalists being groomed at the city's universities. She has often been invited to lecture to them. "The students look at me like I am crazy," she says. "They want good-paying jobs, and for that, with rare exceptions, they will kowtow to whoever will pay them. The profession is now little more than PR."

One daring young journalism student got her message and became her acolyte. When protests erupted in Moscow against the massive fraud in the 2011 parliamentary elections, with tens of thousands taking to the street in Moscow, there was barely a ripple in the provinces and no coverage by the local media. But Mikhail Galyan, an aspiring journalist and photographer, tried to drum up support for a protest meeting in Chelyabinsk using VKontakte, the Russian version of Facebook. The authorities quickly homed in on him. He was called into the dean's office, where three men politely but firmly tried to dissuade him, arguing that Putin and his United Russia supporters had people's interests at heart. He went anyway, joined by a couple thousand people. Many more were disgusted with the blatant election fraud, but most people I spoke to were frightened of appearing in public. One acquaintance flew to Moscow to join the demonstrations, confident that there he would not be identified and suffer repercussions.

Poorly attended and poorly organized, the Chelyabinsk

meeting dissolved into chaos. Anyone could stand up and speak. It turned off many of those who were looking for a political alternative. Across the country, the fractured opposition lacked a compelling message or strategy. Locked out of the mainstream media, it had a small opening when the election protests grew. But it seemed to blow the opportunity, confirming there was no viable replacement for Putin.

As Putin campaigned for the presidency yet again in 2012, a friend of mine—a government employee involved in the arts—quietly ignored her boss's order to attend a pro-Putin rally. In response, her boss punished her for her absence. Her office computer was disconnected from the Internet and her work space left unheated. It could have been worse, she mused. She could have been fired. But the message did not escape those around her.

Any state or private company or institution that receives support from the government must show its support for Putin and his appointees or face cuts. The authorities check the results at polling stations, which are often inside factories, government buildings, or universities, punishing those who don't provide desired results. At a university in Chelyabinsk, voters were required to take their cell phones into the booth and photograph their ballots to show how they had voted. Those who refused could expect repercussions such as the cancellation of their scholarships. Clever students figured out how to get around this. They took in a thread, arranged it next to Putin's name in the shape of a tick, photographed the ballot, and then removed the thread and voted as they wished.

Putin got 60 percent of the vote. Despite fraud and coercion, polls indicate Putin would have won without such shenanigans, though not with such a wide margin. Mikhail Galyan insisted on expressing his anger publicly. He mounted a one-man protest, bicycling around the city with a poster displaying Vladimir Putin dressed as Father Christmas. The image was defaced by a huge *X*, with the words "Winter Is Over." Mikhail admits this message might seem a little obscure, especially to foreigners, but he says he kept it a bit opaque to confound the police. Most important, he thinks the many residents who were used to codes would have understood that what he meant was "It's time for change." The poster referred to what is known as the thaw, when the Soviet leader Nikita Khrushchev relaxed draconian restrictions after the dictator Joseph Stalin died in 1953. Mikhail was trying to say it's time to stop being afraid and speak out. Though he had broken no laws and held no illegal gathering, he and his bike were eventually stopped by a group of policemen. At the very least, they could see that Putin's image had a big X on it. They started haranguing him, asking who had paid him, suggesting he was being bankrolled by the United States. Two "thugs" in civilian clothes appeared and joined in. They threatened to have him killed. When Mikhail turned to the cops demanding they do something, they stood in silence. The "thugs" were clearly Putin's thugs.

Seeing no future for his profession at home, Mikhail Galyan is yet another talented Russian to leave the country and pursue a future in Germany. "I don't believe in any officials," Mikhail told me on Skype. "Maybe there are some individuals who aren't bad, but they are part of a system whose one goal is to keep that system in place." He recalled a quotation from Boris Yeltsin's longtime prime minister, Viktor Chernomyrdin: "We want it to be better, but it always turns out the same." Mikhail's response: "It stays the same because people won't do anything because they think nothing they do will make a difference."

Chelyabinsk is a typical Russian city where everyone knows one another's business. Restrictions on freedom of speech are more severe than in Moscow, where the sheer size of the population provides some with anonymity and the attention of the West provides others with a measure of protection. The Kremlin allows Moscow's independent media a slim degree of editorial freedom, if only to let off steam among those who don't support the status quo. But the zone of permissible utterance is shrinking. The one place where you can still see real fights over Russia's past, present, and future is the blogosphere. It fills in where commercial news organizations fear to tread, and it has been a powerful subversive source enabling scholars, reporters like Irina, and others to bring a wide range of topics to public discussion outside the controlled traditional media. The country's huge community of bloggers still has relatively unfettered access to information from home and abroad, though given the laws now on the books, all this could be easily silenced.

Journalism is at best a complicated beast, but in Russia it is unquestionably a sleazy business, intimidated, co-opted, corrupted, and bought. Alexander Podoprigora, an influential political scientist and blogger in Chelyabinsk, regularly posted detailed charges of wrongdoing against Putin's appointed governor, apparently without fear of recrimination. His posts were widely reposted because it was "safe," clear to everyone he had protection. No one without protection would have dared to publish such material; many believe he was protected by the region's security services. In Russia, it's too often a question not of independent commentary but of who is backing whom. When one read between the lines of the Chelyabinsk media, it was clear there was a battle going on, with the security services and their business partners pitted against the governor and his cronies. In large part thanks to Podoprigora, the governor was so compromised he resigned. Even so, he clearly had his own protectors: he was dispatched to Moscow, where he became a member of parliament with immunity from prosecution.

■

Russia's experiment with press freedom was brief. In the late 1980s, Gorbachev's glasnost policy went much further than he ever imagined. A new community of journalists was determined to uncover a country that had been held under wraps. But who was going to pay the journalists once the state stopped?

Ann Cooper is a former foreign correspondent and a professor of journalism at Columbia University. She has deftly summed up the history of Russian journalism for the Committee to Protect Journalists, explaining how economics rather than journalistic ethics quickly took hold. The new, obscenely rich built media empires that combined investigative reporting with private score settling. By 1996, when President Boris Yeltsin was in a potentially tight race with his Communist opponent, TV journalists dropped any pretense at objectivity, justifying their vilification of the Communists as support for democracy.

When Boris Yeltsin ceded the presidency to Vladimir Putin, the media owners got a new, stricter lesson in loyalty and obedience. The clever satirical programs were shut down. There were to be no more clever barbs at authority and no more investigative journalism. Putin made it clear he would not brook criticism of him or his circle. The country's six national TV stations and their journalists were brought under state control. There was one holdout, the opposition-oriented national TV channel called Dozhd, or "Rain," but in 2014 it too was shackled. Under Kremlin pressure, nearly all cable networks dropped Dozhd, making it available only on the Web for a fee. Meanwhile, landlords, feeling political pressure, evicted the station from its headquarters. Dozhd has struggled to find a new home.

During an interview with Anton Druzhinin, a director for the Russian branch of Emerson Process Management, the American firm that employs more than a thousand in Chelyabinsk, I asked whether he was concerned about the shrinking media landscape. Well traveled, well compensated, multilingual, and savvy, he threw the question back at me. "What's the problem?" he asked, citing Dozhd and Internet sites as evidence there was no problem.

The problem is that most Russians get their news from TV

channels, not from shrinking Internet sites or blogs, and these channels have become shrill purveyors of conspiracy theories and anti-Western propaganda. Gleb Pavlovsky, a political consultant and skilled spin doctor who helped Putin during his first election campaign and remained a Kremlin adviser for years afterward, has lately parted ways. He is concerned about Putin's lack of strategic thinking and the consequences of the feverish anti-Ukrainian, anti-American, and generally xenophobic programming. "This keeps people in a traumatized state," he says. "They lose their sanity. They become paranoid and aggressive."

■

Local TV, which in the 1990s remained somewhat independent of the Kremlin and its oligarchs, is now totally subservient. It is almost exclusively controlled by regional governments dependent on the Kremlin or by industrialists dependent on the authorities' largesse. The so-called independent local media are far from truly independent; they rely on lucrative government contracts that require them to publish official utterances with no critical commentary. Commercial news outlets also depend on business advertising, and it's a rare business that will jeopardize its relationship with the government by supporting opposition voices. News is further tainted by the common Russian practice of writing "for order." News organizations regularly have an office dedicated to this unethical practice, which is a handy source of income. I once read an interesting item and contacted the reporter whose byline it carried. He was embarrassed, finally admitting he had no idea if the story was true because it had been commissioned.

The managing editor of a major Chelyabinsk online news site, who spoke only on condition I did not use his name, says he can't remember the last time his site criticized the government. In general, he says, "we try to avoid conflict"—a nice way of saying he and his owners don't want to offend officials and advertisers or end up in court or worse. The financial penalties for libel and defamation, which are loosely defined by the courts, are crippling.

The editor, who became a journalist during the heady and idealistic 1990s, is yet another member of the profession who is now embarrassed. Censorship is forbidden under the Russian Constitution. What he describes is a nefarious web of self-censorship and self-preservation. When I asked if he reported about people like my friend who was illegally punished for refusing to attend a Putin rally, he said no, though he confessed he knew plenty of people who had suffered the same fate. His sources would not speak out on the record. And if they won't take the responsibility for speaking out, he won't touch a subject. "People are afraid," he explained, and "self-censorship is the greatest evil." He is a perfect example of self-censorship.

With the recent tightening of government control, the country's most popular social networking site, VKontakte, has come under pressure. According to its founder and former CEO Pavel Durov, the FSB ordered him to turn over personal information on activists who took part in the uprising in Kiev. Durov said he refused to comply and was fired. He has fled Russia, claiming VKontakte is now under the full control of Kremlin friends and officials.

Despite its control of the media, the government remains unsatisfied. There is constant discussion in the corridors of power about a supposed glut of negative news that is poisoning the country's image. Some members of parliament even criticize the chastened state TV channels, complaining they would rather cover car crashes than the opening of new factories. If these politicians had their way, there would be a return to the Soviet Union's happy news.

The cultural minister Vladimir Medinsky is just their kind of guy. He had made his name with a series of bestselling revisionist pop history books debunking what he calls "dirty myths" about Russia, largely promulgated by what he calls "Westernizers." He writes that no country has faced so much prolonged demonization as Russia. He has lashed out at Russia's intelligentsia, saying, "It's important that the intellectual elite stop digging into our common past with a view to seeking out only mistakes. Enough self-exposure. Our history is full of great military exploits. This will teach us where to go and what our nation's cause is."

The overwhelming government campaign has targeted not just the media and bloggers but free speech more generally. One of Russia's most beloved rock musicians, Andrei Makarevich, the front man for the group Time Machine, was branded a traitor for his public criticism of Moscow over its policies in Ukraine. Though he was once the recipient of the Kremlin's top awards, his concerts were suddenly canceled under government threats and pressure.

The film and theater director Vladimir Mirzoev was among the few public figures daring to sign an open letter published in the independent newspaper *Novaya Gazeta* protesting the war in Ukraine and what it called Russia's self-isolation and restoration of totalitarianism. Mirzoev's following is among the intellectual elite theatergoing crowd. He poses less of a threat than the rock singer Makarevich and has not been punished.

In his public comments, Mirzoev resorts to psychology to explain the country's intolerant mood. "I understand that our population is deeply traumatized by the entire twentieth century. There are people who can easily fall into a state of maniacal euphoria and patriotic psychosis and just as easily fall into depression. It's a bipolar disorder where people react to generally frightening things in a completely inappropriate way. They deny war is being waged. It's possible of course to say that Russians are a victim of TV propaganda, but after all, it's still not that hard to get on the Internet to find alternative information to compare and contrast the facts. But they don't want to compare anything;

they cannot accept the thought that their country, their homeland, is the aggressor."

Tamara Mairova may be the sort of person Mirzoev has in mind. A retired engineer at a military factory, and highly educated, she is an avid TV watcher, and when confronted with other views over the kitchen table, she defends state television, stubbornly declaring, "Facts are facts." A discussion of events in Ukraine quickly reverts to what she believes is a long-standing attempt by the West to undermine Russia. She remembers watching in despair in the 1990s as her military factory was plundered by others in management, who sold off whatever they could. She recalls, "No one was interested in producing anything, no one was thinking, everyone was stealing." She blames President Boris Yeltsin and his Western advisers. "All those financial manipulations, the rush to privatize, these ideas didn't come from here, they came from you, from the West, but the West didn't have to live through the results."

"But weren't the Russians to blame for the corruption?" I ask her. "Ah yes, we Russians learn quickly," she says, laughing bitterly. "Yes, we Russians adapted in the most creative of ways, but you created the conditions."

Mairova survived by creating a new company to service the oil industry. Before she was crushed again by the financial crisis of 1998, when Russia defaulted on its loans, she had managed to build a large house, constructed in part by engineers and scientists, friends who had lost their jobs and their way. After a childhood in a communal barracks, followed by years in a primitive house, she now has a fortress against future uncertainty. Despite their large home, she and her husband live modestly, eating what they grow in their garden and doing any repairs themselves. She sort of jokingly pretends to fire an automatic weapon, to show that she is ready to defend her Russia from all comers.

Her daughter, in her thirties, takes a much more skeptical view of state information and tried to defend me from both her

mother's overwhelming hospitality and her mother's fury with
the West. She failed on both counts. Tamara regularly talks to
friends in eastern Ukraine, and she fully subscribes to the official
narrative that the separatists are rescuing Russians and Russian
speakers from the depredations of Ukrainian fascists and Western intrigue. She points out that the Ukrainian government has
cut off some of the country's eastern regions from subsidies and
pensions, alienating members of the population who might have
been neutral.

Tamara dismisses any "facts" that contradict her views as
lies from the West. Unfortunately, she is not altogether wrong.
Though not nearly as outrageous as Russian propaganda, Western reporting on Ukraine has been shabby. The Western media
have portrayed what happened in Ukraine as a popular democratic revolt against dictatorship, but it can also be understood
as the unconstitutional overthrow of an elected if frequently thug-
gish government. Western journalists have repeated unsubstantiated and unconfirmed claims by Ukraine's government without
confirmation while being quick to dismiss Russian reports, without checking them. They have underreported the less savory actions of armed Kiev-backed nationalists and paid little attention
to the flaws of the country's "pro-Western" government, such as
its lack of a vision for how to unite the country and its inability to
curb corruption and advance economic reform. All this simply
fuels the worst of Russian propaganda and the difficulty of
reaching a durable negotiated settlement.

When I ask the journalist Irina Gundareva how long Russians
will put up with compromised information, corrupt officials, compliant courts, and a covert war, she just shakes her head and says,
"People want to enjoy today, what is available, after waiting so
long. Everyone is now guilty. Everyone pays bribes. Russians are
patient. They believe the government. Perhaps there will be an
outcry when there is no sausage in the stores, when there are once
again no salaries. I just don't know where the red line is."

In Russia, families and friends have split with each other over the takeover of Crimea and Putin's interference in eastern Ukraine and his demands for loyalty or else. Emotions are so high at times that one friend said, "You see how wonderful a friend can be and how terrifying it is once a friend becomes an enemy." As of early 2015, the balance of opinion remains very much on Putin's side.

Even before events in Ukraine, I had noticed a growing caution among friends to speak openly, and certainly on the phone. The old Soviet phrase "This is not a phone conversation" came back into use. And there was that incident I mentioned earlier when a neighbor allegedly complained that I, a foreigner, was living in the building. I was taken to the police station, where my visa was checked. Initially, the police said it would take an hour, but the hours ticked by. In the meantime, my landlord called to ask if I had left the door open: a police patrol had found it unlocked and called him with an unprecedented offer to fix the lock for free. This was all rather surprising, because I had indeed locked the door of the apartment when I'd left, and it was inconceivable that police patrolling the neighborhood just happened to enter the building and "notice" there was something wrong with the door to my fifth-floor walk-up. It was even more inconceivable that the police would offer to call a locksmith and ask him to fix the lock for free.

Later that evening, I happened to be attending an English-language club, which regularly meets at the local university. I mentioned what had happened. Would someone call the police about a foreigner in their midst? "Oh no, that could not happen," said one young woman, adding, "We all hate the police, and no one would ever denounce someone." Later, quietly, another young woman told me to be careful, noting that her grandparents had been denounced by their neighbors and that nothing since Stalin's times had really changed.

The assembled were members of a group called Speak Freely,

so named a few years ago when speaking freely was the norm. It now means "speak English to the best of your ability on neutral subjects." When the meeting was officially over, a few members approached me, away from the others, to give me their best guess of what had happened. They suggested that I had been deliberately lured to the police station so that investigators, sure of my whereabouts, could then break into the apartment and look at my belongings, including my computer. They posited that the incompetent investigators could not figure out how to relock the door when they left, requiring the call to the landlord with the strange offer to fix the lock.

SIXTEEN

NUCLEAR NIGHTMARE

Chelyabinsk is the birthplace of the Soviet Union's nuclear program, the Russian equivalent of Hanford in Washington State or Oak Ridge in Tennessee. As the historian Kate Brown makes searingly clear in her book *Plutopia*, the Soviet and American nuclear programs both skimped on safety and waste management to prioritize production. They both repressed information about accidents, forging safety records and glossing over sick workers, but the results in Chelyabinsk were incomparable. Tens of thousands were doomed to radioactive poisoning, with others left to wonder what their fate might be. Thousands of acres have been affected. While the Chernobyl accident topped any one event, the cumulative impact in Chelyabinsk of repeated accidents, combined with years of secrecy, has earned this region the unwanted reputation of "the most contaminated place on the planet."

In 1945, Joseph Stalin chose an isolated corner of the Chelyabinsk region as the site for his new nuclear weapons program. A thousand miles from Moscow and a hundred miles from the regional capital, it was far from prying eyes but close enough to maintain adequate communications. The area's forests provided building materials, and its pristine rivers and lakes offered the necessary water supply.

Following the defeat of Nazi Germany, the Soviet Union was devastated. Large parts of the country had been leveled. Poverty was widespread, and there was a dearth of scientific and technical specialists. Spurred by the American use of nuclear weapons against Japan, the Soviet Union rushed to build its own bomb, devouring scarce resources. It did not succeed as fast as it wanted, but it still built a bomb in a staggeringly short time. Speed led to repeated accidents, a lack of concern for safety and health, overwhelming pollution, illness, and death. Some have argued, "We saved the Soviet Union: it was worth it." Others believe the price was too high.

The nuclear program eventually came under the so-called Ministry of Medium Machine Building, a deliberately innocuous name to mask the furious secret activity. The initial construction was done by Soviet prison labor, German prisoners of war, and young conscripts. Despite often frigid conditions, they lived in tents and trenches. In two years, the number of workers exploded to forty-seven thousand. They knew the place only by its postal address—first Chelyabinsk 40, later changed to Chelyabinsk 65. The plutonium-processing plant would eventually be called Mayak, meaning "lighthouse."

The initial project was an experimental reactor. Primitive even by the standards of the day, it looked like a vast brick beehive. The next step was to build the first of four industrial graphite reactors, which went into operation by 1948. Along with this, there was a chemical plant for the extraction of plutonium from the uranium irradiated in the reactor and a metallurgical plant to convert the plutonium concentrate to high-purity metallic plutonium for the first Soviet atomic bomb.

The inaugural industrial reactor quickly had serious problems, and to save the valuable uranium blocks inside, workers removed them with their bare hands. For a little extra food, soldiers also cleaned highly radioactive waste with rags and a bucket. Unbeknownst to them, they were getting in ten to twelve minutes more than what would even then have been considered a permissible annual dose of radiation.

Brigades rotated through again and again and were regularly exposed to unacceptable radiation levels. When the soldiers and prisoners were eventually released, there was no record of where they had been or what they had been exposed to. If they fell ill in their homes far away, doctors had no way to diagnose them. Their subsequent illnesses and deaths are not recorded.

Vladimir Chervinsky, forced to work at the plant in 1951, describes a total disregard for conscripts: "When we asked why we were getting sick, they told us fresh air would cure us when the work was over. Cure us of what they did not say." After nine months at the nuclear facility, he was let go, with no documentation, and given no compensation.

Soldiers and prisoners were the first to die. Other cases of acute radiation sickness occurred in the factory, where a predominantly female workforce separated plutonium from radioactive uranium by hand. The academic I. V. Petrianov-Sokolov recalled how sick the women there looked, noting there were not even the most elementary safety rules. Many died before they reached their thirties.

Doctors were ordered to the nuclear complex in 1949 to diagnose and treat the growing numbers with radiation sickness. Dr. Mira Kosenko, who was hired much later but knew many of the early physicians who worked there, has carefully and painfully documented the early history. She describes how doctors were brought to Chelyabinsk 40 in cars with the windows blacked out so they could not know the route. They could not communicate with their families. In some cases, their relatives assumed they had been arrested and sent to labor camps.

The first medical staff had no training in radiation sickness, and because of secrecy it had no right to attend international or domestic conferences on the subject. As Dr. Angelina Guskova, one of the first doctors on-site, optimistically put it, "We learned by trial and success." But it was not easy to save their patients. When doctors tried to remove clearly irradiated people from the workplace, their requests were met with condescension from superiors who said their diagnoses were "the fantasy of inexperienced boys and girls." Officials did not want to lose experienced workers. Guskova, who recognized that the workers were regularly being overdosed, had to fight for each one she removed from work. She later said, "I am very proud we succeeded and were able to return 90 percent to health." But how long that health continued is unclear, given the inadequate follow-up and records.

Soon after the start of the program, yet another problem arose—what to do with the radioactive waste. For four years, workers dumped large quantities of highly contaminated waste into the nearby Techa River, which flowed past forty villages, where twenty-eight thousand people lived at the time. It is narrow, sometimes no more than the width of a sidewalk. It's also slow moving, so much of the waste collected in the banks and bottom sediment. The river wends its way for 150 miles until it flows into another river system that eventually reaches the Arctic Sea. The villages along its shore had always been poor agricultural communities, made up of Russians and local ethnic groups—the Muslim Tatars and Bashkirs. These people depended on the river for drinking, for watering their fields, for washing clothes, for swimming and fishing. In 1990, when Dr. Mira Kosenko was finally able to ask high-ranking officials why they did nothing to protect people they knew were dependent on the river, they lamely answered they thought the radioactive waste would all dissolve and disappear. It didn't, and they knew it wouldn't.

In 1951, river measurements were finally taken after radiation was detected a thousand miles away in Russia's Arctic waters. Along the Techa, there were dramatically high radiation levels not only in the river but in the soil and fields where villagers kept their cows and chickens.

In Metlino, the first village downstream from the point of release, residents accumulated the highest radiation doses: four hundred to six hundred times the normal annual exposure to radioactive isotopes. Others farther downstream also accumulated high doses. Despite this, the use of river water was forbidden only in 1952, a full year after testing and four years after the dumping began. Given the secrecy of the program, villagers along the Techa weren't given reasons to stop using the river, which was their lifeblood. They had no alternatives because most didn't have wells.

Soon enough, residents showed signs of dizziness, nausea, the impairment of red blood cells, and a decrease in white cells. Leukemia and other cancers followed. The government decided to relocate certain villages, but the evacuation was repeatedly delayed. Because of the secrecy of the nuclear program, the villagers were given no explanation for their peremptory eviction, adding trauma to their already poor health. Villagers were forced from where they had lived for generations and where their ancestors were buried. They left their homes, with almost no compensation, for far worse housing.

The evacuation of villages stopped in 1957 when a Soviet official announced the Techa River was safe. According to Dr. Kosenko, "The recommendation of one man brought disaster for thousands of people left behind, but it was in the interest of the nuclear program and so it was taken." Funds for relocation had been diverted elsewhere.

Bad as things were, the biggest troubles were yet to come. On September 29, 1957, the monitoring system gauging heat in a radioactive waste containment storage tank at the Mayak processing plant failed. The tank exploded. Most of the debris fell close to the explosion site, where on that first night dosimeters showed radiation levels were forty thousand times the accepted levels. The rest formed a radioactive cloud over an area the size of New Jersey. The Soviet authorities kept this secret from those living in its path and from the rest of the world.

Once again construction teams, largely made up of conscripts, took the brunt. No fewer than twenty thousand soldiers were called in to clean up the 1957 accident. There is no information about the doses they received, and once again their fate is unknown. According to Dr. Mira Kosenko, "When the soldiers were freed from service, the state freed itself of concern about them."

Remaining villages, which had already been contaminated by the Techa, were once again the victims. Authorities dithered for ten days over whether to move the residents or not. Iran Khaerzamanov describes how his ten-month-old daughter, caught in the cloud, died a few days later, throwing up blood. Other children were sick. He says adults survived better. Soldiers arrived in their village and killed all the dogs and cats as a preamble to evacuation. Then they killed the cows and flocks of chickens and geese. "Everyone was crying, and rumors spread that after the animals were gone, they were going to kill us," he recalls. "There was total panic." The villagers were ordered to sit in their houses for another ten days, and when they were finally moved, they could take almost nothing. They were ordered to burn most of their belongings before they were transferred to a distant village where their new shelter was little more than plywood shells. Once again they were given no explanation.

In the 1960s, Dr. Mira Kosenko was hired by a new institute that was to study and treat the radiation cases. She had wanted to continue her work as a research cardiologist, but her "biography" worked against her: her father had been sent to the camps in 1937, accused of anti-Soviet activity, and her mother was Jewish. She hardly thought she was a candidate for a job in a secret medical institution, about which she was told very little, but as she puts it, "Fate works in strange ways."

Kosenko and her colleagues tried to do the best they could

with limited resources. Medicines and blood were in short supply. The distance between their clinic and the villages they were trying to help was another impediment. What passed for roads were rutted pathways. In the summer months, they would set up makeshift medical centers in local schools, taking with them everything from mattresses and sheets to lab equipment and fresh water, which locals certainly did not have. Under strict state secrecy laws, they were not allowed to inform their patients about their exposure or of any diagnosis related to radiation, compounding their confusion and future contamination.

Because there were such poor records, it was difficult to figure out which illnesses were from long-term radiation and which were simply a result of impoverished living conditions and rampant infectious diseases. Symptoms are often interchangeable. One thing was clear: the health of the local people was bad.

As Kosenko and her colleagues tried to cope with the legacy of the Mayak accident, irresponsible authorities added new cases to their load. Local children were ordered to dismantle buildings in contaminated villages. Neither they nor their parents were informed about the risks, and no one was there to check on radiation levels and doses.

There was yet another devastating accident. Once the authorities "officially" stopped dumping large quantities of waste into the Techa River, they stored it in nearby Lake Karachay. Really more a bog than a lake, it was chosen because it had no outlet. But highly radioactive material nonetheless leached into the underlying water table. Then, during the long hot summer of 1967, Karachay dried up and strong winds dispersed highly radioactive dust across a vast territory, affecting thousands of new victims as well as those who had already been repeatedly contaminated.

It was only in 1989, under pressure from the new environmental movement, that the Ministry of Medium Machine Building released a thick pamphlet about Mayak's accidents. Allowed a rare visit to the area, the American scientist Thomas Cochran estimated Karachay still contained two and a half times the total release from the Chernobyl accident. He concluded that a person standing on the shores of Karachay would accumulate a lethal dose of radiation within an hour.

The growing antinuclear movement forced the declassification of the formerly secret health clinics in the region. Natalia Mironova helped a family successfully sue for damages, resulting in an incredible admission by Russian authorities of the link between Mayak's emissions and genetic damage. She hoped environmental injustices of the past would finally be redressed. But according to Kate Brown, the then president, Boris Yeltsin, backed away from his support for environmental activists when they were no longer useful to him in his campaign to discredit his foes in the Communist Party. The environmentalists had now become the enemy, threatening to expose Mayak and his government to phenomenal liabilities. Subsequent petitioners lost case after case.

In 1994, Russia's secret nuclear weapons cities finally appeared on maps. In Chelyabinsk, this included Snezhinsk, where the Schurs live, and the plutonium-processing complex, which got the new name of Ozersk—drawn from the Russian word for "lake." These benign appellations have done little to stop controversy and suspicion. Accidents in Ozersk have continued, with authorities trying to hush them up. The early activists like Natalia Mironova came under increasing pressure to stay quiet. Mironova was accused of treason and financially crippled by Putin's tax police. Even so, she inspired others to keep up their work.

Nadezhda Kutepova didn't join Mironova's antinuclear movement when it first appeared in the late 1980s and early 1990s. She was busy becoming a nurse, having her first children, and struggling to get by. Like so many, she was frantically buying goods and bringing them to Ozersk to resell, one of the few ways to earn a living. A Julia Roberts look-alike, she tried modeling.

She went to night school to get a sociology degree. Finally, around 2000, when her life was at a crossroads, a friend suggested she go to an environmental human rights meeting. She grudgingly agreed. Everything came together: her family history, her search for a meaningful career, and a group of committed activists. She was hooked. In 2004, she set up her own NGO, the Planet of Hopes, based in Ozersk, her hometown. She has depended on grants from U.S. and European funders. Though she does not have a formal legal degree, she has taught herself to be an advocate for the thousands who, like her family, have been denied compensation and recognition.

Kutepova was born in 1972, when Ozersk was still known only by its postal code. She describes herself as an ordinary Soviet girl, except that many people in or around her family had died early or become disabled. "I thought this was normal. The question 'why' did not occur to me." Her grandmother was a chemical engineer who worked in the most dangerous part of the Mayak complex and died young of cancer. Her father died young of lung cancer. As a nineteen-year-old, he had been rounded up along with thousands of others to be "liquidators," those who cleaned up after the 1957 accident. Years later, when he died, there was no way to prove his death was related to radiation exposure. There were incomplete records showing who had taken part in the cleanup, and his name didn't show up.

Those who have come to Kutepova for help include the children and pregnant women who were forced to be "liquidators." They were theoretically banned from such work and therefore not included on any official rosters. According to Kutepova, "Many victims in Russia still can't receive compensation for a nuclear accident that happened more than fifty years ago." She bitterly notes, "The Russian government seems to want to wait until all the victims have died. Then they might decide to pay compensation, but since they will all be dead, the state will pay nothing at all. If we succeed in helping victims of the past, it will be a great help to those who suffer today and are still afraid to speak up."

In the middle of the first decade of the twenty-first century, officials searched Kutepova's office and home without a warrant. They accused her of tax evasion, a typical tactic used against human rights activists, but the case was eventually dropped. Officials then turned up at her child's kindergarten, asking pointed questions about her suitability as a mother. This was clearly another threat.

When Kutepova tried to launch a sociological study of life in closed cities, along with a respected St. Petersburg academic, they were accused of espionage. Once again all charges were subsequently dropped, but the study was unable to go forward. Officials continue to call her in for "friendly" interviews, warning that her work could have "unfortunate results."

As a result of dogged investigation, she and other environmental activists uncovered a closed court ruling in which it was revealed that the Mayak nuclear-processing plant had continued to dump radioactive waste into the Techa River from 2001 to 2004. It had taken five years to get access to the sealed information. Despite repeated denials by Mayak officials, the judge determined that "increases in background radiation caused danger to the residents' health and lives, including acute myeloid leukemia and other types of cancer." The judge also noted that funds for cleanup had been diverted to bonuses. Kutepova also succeeded in showing that Mayak officials had falsified information about yet another accident.

Kutepova has been furiously litigious. Though her success in court has not been overwhelming, she continues to fight for victims' compensation, document the continued contamination, and report human rights violations in the closed nuclear cities. In 2015, the Ministry of Justice added her name to the growing list of "foreign agents," ignoring her contention that she was involved in civic activity, not political work. Because she had not registered first as a foreign agent, a label she disputes, she faces crippling fines.

Perhaps the most complicated and emotional issue has been the fate of five riverside villages that were never evacuated in the 1950s, though in some cases they were just two hundred yards from those villages that were moved. Most of those left behind were Bashkir or Tatar—a fact that has led over the years to charges of ethnic genocide. Though there is no evidence to support this thesis, many residents believe the authorities deliberately ignored their villages, despite the dangers, so they could be guinea pigs in an experiment to measure the effects of long-term radiation exposure.

Whatever the reasons these villages were left behind, residents feel that they have been victimized. While dismissed as rubes, they have charted their families' demise. They know when they look around them that they and their family members are sick, and sick in unusual ways.

Tight-knit communities, bound by family and poverty, they can't move, because no one would buy their houses or land. The system of compensation that has evolved is seemingly arbitrary, with some villagers getting a stipend, albeit only twelve dollars a month, while their immediate neighbors get nothing. When they have complained, the authorities have dismissed their health issues as nothing more than the result of alcoholism and called them opportunists looking for a handout. Scientists have long understood that radioactive isotopes can have disparate effects on the body. The inherent complexity of diagnosis has made it easy for both American and Russian leaders to deny any ill effects.

■

In 2005, the federal government finally set in motion a plan to resettle Muslyumovo, one of the five remaining villages. A relatively big village, it sprawled inside a bend in the Techa River. It was never relocated, at least in part because of its size and because Soviet contractors maintained it would be too expensive to rebuild. By 1999, a local doctor estimated that 95 percent of the infants born here had genetic disorders, while 90 percent suffered anemia, fatigue, and immune disorders.

When officials finally broached the move, many residents wanted to get as far away as they could, to clean suburban areas outside the regional capital. But officials deemed that option too expensive and complicated. Instead, the local government picked a spot, on the other side of the river, less than two miles away, which raised questions about just how safe it was. Residents were also given the option of taking the equivalent of thirty-seven thousand dollars to buy a new home somewhere else. But who got that money? In many houses, there were several generations crammed in together, victims of poor health and an absence of jobs in a place no one wanted to be. It was determined the total payment would be thirty-seven thousand dollars per house no matter whether one person lived there or ten. The system was a mess. Payment for those wishing to leave was often not forthcoming, and when it was, it was not enough to buy anything comparable.

Those living in the other remaining villages have not even been given such choices. They continue to survive along the Techa, and as Nikolai Oshurkov, a village official in Brodokalmak, described it, the legacy of isolation, poverty, and the fear of radioactive contamination has cursed them.

When I drove out there in 2012, the road to Brodokalmak was ornamented with posters of President Putin's appointed governor, an extremely wealthy businessman, asking people to live "decently." As I turned off toward the village and the Techa, the road turned to mud. There used to be a state farm here, but Oshurkov pointed around, saying, "Look, now it's totally destroyed, a ruin." The village community has fallen apart, divided by conflicting reports that the river is safe or the river is deadly. There's no private enterprise, no tax base, and no jobs.

Far from getting compensation, the village has been strangled by the regional government, which has fined it for not complying with impossible regulations. Meanwhile, half the dilapidated wooden houses have no access to gas for heat, and almost half have no running water. Oshurkov says what really galls him is that "regional officials don't give a shit."

The mayor talked with an Israeli businessman who wanted to start a chicken farm here, promising him favorable conditions. After learning about the village history, the investor backed out. Though he would not have to use the river water, he said the region's reputation would kill his business. "I can just hear it," he told the mayor, "I deal in radioactive chickens." That was the last experience with potential investors. Despite offers of free land to businesses, Nikolai Oshurkov says there are no takers.

Down from a high of ten thousand, three thousand people, including young families, still live here. Why? I ask. Oshurkov struggles to answer: "It's our home; we are loyal to this place. Our grandparents lived here, our parents. And since no one is going to buy our houses, where are we supposed to go?" Though he has sent his children away, he says it's extremely difficult for most village kids to find their way in the cities.

At the local school, the teacher Valentina Pashnina has created a museum, including a small room dedicated to Mayak and how it affected the Techa and Brodokalmak. A tiny, feisty woman, with unnaturally purple hair, she was one of the first to read the newspapers and collect information on what had happened. But at the time, she says, the farm was dissolving. There were no salaries, and people were desperate. The shock of the contamination, she says, was just one of many.

She regularly carries a dosimeter and registers "hot spots" where radiation levels are several times the norm. There's nothing she can do about it. "We are hostages," she says. She too has sent her children away. "There is nothing here," she concludes, adding, "There is actually worse than nothing."

In the closed city of Ozersk, home to the Mayak weapons complex and the source of so much pain, living conditions are much better. I was not permitted to enter, but from firsthand descriptions and satellite photographs it has developed from nothing in the late 1940s to a relatively attractive if boring Russian city. Like Snezhinsk, the closed nuclear city where the Schurs live, salaries have dramatically improved, and the fear that disgruntled, impoverished nuclear scientists might smuggle out some weapons-grade material is much less than before. As one U.S. official put it, "The concern is less desperation than opportunism."

Like Russia's nine other closed nuclear cities, scattered across the country, Ozersk and the Mayak complex remain surrounded by a double fence of chain-link barbed wire and tight security. The city remains shut off to all but residents, workers, and suppliers with special passes. To get a relative inside for a family celebration takes a month-and-a-half advance notice, unless, of course, you are an official, in which case the screening takes but a few days.

According to U.S. experts, corruption is now the biggest threat to Russia's nuclear security. Several officials in charge of nuclear weapons or sensitive materials have been arrested for taking bribes. Local government officials in Ozersk have repeatedly been removed for corruption.

Mayak no longer makes plutonium, due to a U.S.-Russian agreement to stop all new plutonium production. But it now houses weapons-grade plutonium from thousands of decommissioned bombs. The Fissile Material Storage Facility is a fortress with walls twenty-three feet thick, designed to withstand earthquakes and airplane crashes. It was paid for by both the United States and Russia, with Washington contributing more than $300 million.

After ten years of political, bureaucratic, and financial setbacks, its completion in 2003 represented a milestone in U.S.-Russian cooperation, though the Russians have never confirmed how much plutonium has been deposited there and where the residue might be. The United States also worked with the Russians to modernize and improve accounting systems and the security of the weapons-grade nuclear materials stored at Mayak, with Washington providing equipment, expertise, and training.

U.S. experts say it was never easy to judge how successful their efforts were, because the Russians were loath to share information. In the early days of cooperation, the handful of U.S. officials allowed into Ozersk for inspections would take a translator and wander around the downtown, visiting shops. They would schmooze with people in the nuclear facilities' cafeterias and keep their eyes open for small but invaluable details that some experts argue were more useful than anything satellite imagery could reveal. Gradually, on-the-ground access was restricted more and more. U.S. officials could no longer simply chat with people on the street. They were not allowed to carry dosimeters to check radiation levels and were barred from bringing any electronic equipment into the city.

By 2014, Russian and American specialists had agreed there were still eleven sensitive processing sites in Mayak that needed security upgrades, but cooperation was fraying. Despite opposition from many nuclear experts, who argued any cooperation was better than nothing, the U.S. Congress blocked new funds for joint nuclear security projects. The Russians then blocked all access to Mayak and most other closed nuclear installations. Despite this, experts say agreements for cooperation are still in place, should the sides find a way to reengage.

Instead of producing plutonium, Mayak is now involved in other nuclear projects involving sensitive materials. Perhaps the most important is the reprocessing of spent nuclear fuel from Russian reactors and nuclear submarines, as well as the fuel from Soviet-built reactors in countries like Vietnam, Poland, the Czech Republic, and Bulgaria. Mayak is also under contract to reprocess fuel from the controversial Bushehr nuclear plant in Iran. There are plans to build dozens of nuclear power reactors for domestic use and export abroad, but even those wishing to strike commercial deals with Mayak have been denied what they consider necessary access to determine the safety and efficiency of the complex.

A big part of Russia's sales pitch to foreign customers is the promise to reprocess the spent fuel from their nuclear reactors, even though this is a process that results in a great deal of radioactive waste, the fate of which remains unclear. Ignoring this fact, the region's officials have argued that reprocessing spent fuel is a win-win prospect for Chelyabinsk, promising they will "give back the reprocessed products and only money will be left behind."

SEVENTEEN

CHANGING LANDSCAPES

If you were to take a helicopter ride over Russia's countryside, you might think a war had recently ravaged the landscape. The former state and collective farms, each of which employed hundreds against all economic sense, are in ruins. After a U.S. farmer visited a farm in Chelyabinsk in the 1990s, when 450 were still employed there, he told his Russian host the only way to make it in the modern world was to reduce the workforce to at most 40. Instead of a gradual reduction, the farms simply collapsed. Two decades after the end of Communist rule, one-third of the country's arable land lies fallow. Barns and sheds have been left to rot and are little more than eerie skeletons. Many of the picturesque, if crude, one-story log houses with carved shutters now list to one side, as if they are as drunk as the remaining aging inhabitants.

A chopper ride over the northern part of the region reveals charming lakes, nestled in the low-forested Urals. It also reveals trails of smoke from areas blighted by years of uncontrolled industrial and radioactive pollution. The village of Karabash is built around a vast copper mine with its smelters and resulting hills of slag. With no pollution controls for much of its one-hundred-year history, Karabash is yet another site in the Chelyabinsk region that competes for the prize of "the world's most polluted" place. Oversaturated with iron, the river runs yellow in summer and turns bright orange when iced over in winter. The surrounding land has been scorched by acid rain. The local mountain has completely lost its forest cover. The words "Save and Preserve" have been arranged in stones, a bleak call for help. The devastation and the impact on health were so extreme, with the local life expectancy estimated at less than fifty, that the mine was closed in 1990. Those who could moved elsewhere, and the population dropped by half to fifteen thousand. The mine was reopened in 1998 with a new owner, the Russian Copper Company. It insists it has taken measures to clean up the smelters, but environmental monitors say not nearly enough has been done. Whatever the facts, which are disputed, Karabash continues to look like a moonscape.

Environmental groups, like many civic organizations, were inspired and supported by Western NGOs in the early post-Soviet days. Once popular, they have since failed to get the support of most of the region's inhabitants because they are easily frightened off and because those inhabitants are worried about the future of their one-industry towns and the loss of jobs.

After taking advantage of a burst of openness, Western funding, and access to information, environmentalists are now struggling and have had trouble employing official records to support their case. In the city of Chelyabinsk, there are eight monitoring stations that the government set up in Soviet times. They were designed to identify nine sources of pollution, but according to the activist Andrei Talevlin the air is now contaminated by more than one hundred dangerous pollutants, so the official results, when available, "are less than useless." The head of In Defense of the Environment, Talevlin points out that by law the government has to give any plant advance notice of a specific test; this gives operators at government-friendly industries plenty of time to get their act together.

Talevlin, a lawyer, has been a longtime environmentalist and continues to receive modest funding from Norway. He says his organization does not have the means to do sophisticated monitoring on a regular basis. Following long-standing complaints, the local prosecutor brought in an independent laboratory to check levels, and it determined emissions in Chelyabinsk city were extremely dangerous. Even then, the prosecutor failed to bring the polluters to justice. A judge rejected the findings. According to Talevlin, "All judges are named in one form or another by Putin."

In 2015, as he battled the Russian Copper Company's plans to open another huge open-pit mine near the already-polluted regional capital of Chelyabinsk, he too was placed on the list of "foreign agents" and threatened with crippling fines. Despite his standing as one of the region's most effective and responsible environmentalists, he has been locked out of a new civic-government environmental commission, which is stacked with industrialists. Far from being a hysterical activist, he has worked in the most diplomatic and legal ways, trying to bring opposing sides together to discuss issues of community concern. One such meeting was broken up by the police, who claimed there was a bomb threat, a typical ruse used across the country to stymie public discourse. He has despaired of the polarization, writing on his blog, "We have completely stopped listening to one another."

The contradiction between the public's concerns about pollution and the lack of community action is stark. Ask any resident who lives in one of the many industrial towns in Chelyabinsk about pollution, and he or she will say the same thing. It builds up over the weekend, when engineers at the factories are off, and by Monday morning the air is unbearable. Over the 2014 New Year's holiday, the blanket of choking smog in the regional capital was so extreme the authorities warned people not to go outside. Face masks jumped in price. It got even worse during the winter of 2015. Finally, a record twenty thousand residents in the city joined an Internet campaign to say "enough." Watching and smelling the surges of smoke from local plants and fed up with mealymouthed explanations, they went over the heads of local administrators, begging President Putin to do something.

Though some areas have escaped pollution, the regional government's idea of attracting far-flung tourists to a notoriously contaminated area seems somewhat far-fetched. Expensive efforts to remove or limit references to Chelyabinsk's pollution history from the Internet have not been successful. Just type in "Chelyabinsk," and its unwanted reputation is still among the first things to pop up. Locals, however, looking for a cheap getaway see everything in relative terms. If you live in Karabash or the regional capital, a drive to what appears to be a pristine lake is literally a breather. Several ski resorts are in development, with plans to expand one into an elite year-round vacation complex.

As ever, such development schemes provide opportunities for corruption, though the region's new governor has taken some encouraging steps. A former steel plant manager who was initially appointed by Putin, he was subsequently voted in with no serious competitors. He has since challenged the developers who acquire state land for cheap and then sell it for many times more. The governor says he intends to redeem stolen money and bolster the shrinking budget. Many people can't help but ask, "Is this just another war between business groups, known as clans, or a real effort to change the rules of the game?"

Ten miles beyond the sprawling regional capital, you reach villages that are turning into helter-skelter suburbs. A four-story mansion rises up next to a one-story cement two-family house, abutted by a renovated slum. There is no zoning to speak of, except bribes, and no sense of community. In the chaos that still exists twenty-plus years after the end of Soviet rule, it's unclear who is responsible for what when it comes to communal services. Municipalities depend on the regional government for funding and have little or no say about where that money goes.

Drive farther south through the region and remote villages look exactly as they did more than a hundred years ago, with no running water, with communal water pumps, and with mounds of wood, stolen from the local forests, providing the only source of heat. When I tell people I live in a village three hours from New York City, they look at me with a mixture of sympathy, horror, and curiosity. It's one thing to have a rustic house for weekends, but to live in a settlement that Russians associate with potholes, no amenities, no stores, and no pride of place is altogether something else. When I tell them that our excellent library relies on public donations and our ambulance and fire service are staffed by volunteers, there is utter incomprehension. "What?" said one Russian friend. "I wouldn't dream of donating money to my village, because it will be stolen!" Whatever sense of community the "collective" once enforced is gone. Everyone is out for himself. Everyone now lives behind high fences, suspicious of neighbors and the local government, which is dependent on the regional government and ultimately on the Kremlin. But no one is protesting.

In the late 1980s, a prominent Soviet journalist came to the United States for a conference. In those years of desperate shortages, he brought a long list of everything he needed to buy for friends and relatives. His host, however, whisked him away from Boston to the wilds of Vermont for his one free weekend. He was angry, thinking of all the shopping he needed to do. Reassurances that he could buy everything he needed along the way did nothing to calm him. After all, he knew what the countryside was like. When he was taken into a mall, where he purchased everything on his list, he was shocked. He knew American cities were much better stocked than Soviet ones, but he thought villages everywhere had to be the same. Once he had seen the American countryside, he concluded in despair that his country could never catch up.

Thirty minutes outside Chelyabinsk city, five former state farm managers saw opportunity despite all the obstacles. They decided to go out on their own and become private farmers. They were of German descent, like many in Chelyabinsk's villages. Their forebears had been lured to Russia in centuries past, but when World War II broke out, they were considered potential spies and were either arrested or forcibly relocated far from the front. When the Soviet Union was no more, these five farmers didn't want to emigrate, but they did take advantage of training programs the German government offered its Russian kinsmen. They spent several months in Europe, working on farms. They returned to Chelyabinsk hoping to replicate what they had seen in the West.

The earth here can be startlingly dark and rich—it is part of Russia's "black earth zone"—but the growing season is short, and the rainfall far more uncertain than what Europeans enjoy. That is Russia's curse. The best land is not blessed with the best climatic conditions, and like everywhere, those conditions are changing unpredictably. These farmers had to start from scratch. They had nothing but their new knowledge, their determination, and their dreams. In their first year back, as they watched most of their fellow farmers fail, they realized there was no way they could survive on their own, so they pooled their efforts.

Twenty years later, their joint venture, Ilinka, has survived. Bit by bit, these farmers bought up or rented abandoned land. Fields had quickly reverted to incipient forest with trees sprouting everywhere, so it took a huge amount of labor to restore them for agriculture. They couldn't acquire enough land to make a go of grain, and they didn't have the equipment, so they started producing vegetables. They installed irrigation. They put everything they had back into the land. They built primitive storage facilities so they wouldn't have to sell their produce for cheap right out of the fields. Their experience in Europe had taught them how to play the market, such as it was, but they were constantly squeezed by corrupt and unsympathetic officials. Eventually, they were able to buy improved Russian tractors at a fraction of what foreign imports cost. Other domestically produced equipment became available as well, cutting their expenses. When asked what he still has to buy from abroad, Ilinka's director, Aleksei Lipp, doesn't miss a beat: "Combines and seeds." Lipp says the West could undermine Russia overnight if it banned the sale of seeds.

Lipp bought government-backed insurance, given the uncertain weather in Chelyabinsk. One spring, his fields were flooded. A stack of documents a foot high sits on his desk. That, he says, is all he got for it. It was impossible to prove what his losses were, and he implies the insurance plan was just another scam, a way for government officials to make money. He says he would have been smarter putting the wasted money back into the farm. He won't buy government insurance again.

Knowing what it's taken, Aleksei Lipp says he would never try to be a farmer again, and he doesn't want his children to follow in his footsteps. But he's in it now for better or worse. He and his partners recently sold out to an agribusiness firm and are now once again employees. It was the only way to get the necessary investment to grow. Ilinka can now cater to a more discerning public that no longer wants muddy produce. The farm has acquired equipment to wash and package its vegetables, and it plans to create its own brand. Asked about a small but emerging demand for organic vegetables, Lipp laughs and says, "We still don't have money for fertilizers, so you could say we are organic by default."

These farmers plan to turn their experience into a new business. They are moving into IT: they hope to link the struggling farmers in the region with each other and help them develop and manage the services they need, everything from obtaining rental equipment to legal aid, financing, and marketing—whatever they don't have.

Russian agriculture is slowly emerging from the ruins of the 1990s. Regulations on land purchases have been eased. Mikhail

Yurevich, the former governor, mysteriously became the owner of a former state pasta factory, scooping up thousands of acres in the more fertile south of the region and making a fortune as the country's "macaroni king." Russia is now again a grain exporter, though unpredictable and unreliable. Yield per acre is still much lower than in the West and subject to either drought or flooding. The government has repeatedly interfered with big export deals, imposing restrictions to protect domestic supply and prices, at the expense of grain farmers. They are not happy constituents, nor are vegetable farms like Ilinka. They are getting way more for their produce because of Putin's sanctions on European goods, but the cost of their inputs and loans have soared, so at best it's a wash.

The government has suddenly promised all sorts of incentives and subsidies for farmers producing for the domestic market, calling recent bans on Western imports "a golden opportunity for Russian agriculture." Along with its many pledges to cut dependence on imports, the Kremlin wants to make the country self-sufficient in food by 2020. Farmers say the help, given the strained government budget, is coming late or not at all. They warn that upping production is a matter of sustained support over the long term.

One challenge is attracting agronomists and veterinarians willing to live in what are still primitive conditions. The government has promised to provide construction materials so farms like Ilinka can build decent housing for the specialists they need. The biggest issue of all is finding sober field workers who know how to run and maintain agricultural machinery. Young Russians don't want to work for the low wages and long hours and look to the neighboring cities and towns where just about any job will pay more. Because Russia has a tiny population given its objectives, they can find alternatives to farm labor, however modest.

Ilinka and other farms have to rely on Tajiks and Uzbeks—cheap immigrant labor from the poorest of the former Soviet republics. But quotas are getting tighter on non-Russian foreign labor, especially from predominantly Muslim republics.

A few miles away from Aleksei Lipp and Ilinka, Chinese migrants have set up shop, converting acres of unused land into crude greenhouses made of strips of raw wood and plastic sheeting, where they grow tomatoes and cucumbers in the summer months. According to their Russian neighbors, these seasonal Chinese workers live in the greenhouses against all regulations, chop the wood with no restrictions, and pay nothing for the water they use.

The Chinese peasants, who come for six months a year, are more than willing to make the journey in cramped train cars across Siberia from Manchuria, a trek toward economic opportunity familiar to countless Mexicans in California. They make much more than at home and more with their greenhouses than they would if they worked as hired labor on Russian farms. Local farmers, who can't find labor, have protested against this unfair competition. A representative from the Chelyabinsk Ministry of Agriculture, who accompanied me one day, did not deny the Chinese were operating outside the law but was at a loss to explain why. The why, given corruption, was pretty clear. And now that Russia is increasingly dependent on China, as an alternative to the West, one can anticipate the Chinese will be forgiven much more, if not by the locals.

While Russian media reports often warn that the Chinese are taking over Russia's Far East, the Chinese represent only a small segment of Russia's migrant population. A successful Chinese businessman in Chelyabinsk, who started from scratch with a restaurant several years ago, says peasants may come here on a seasonal basis, but he can no longer lure Chinese engineers or skilled laborers to work in his new shoe and furniture factories because they can make more in China—a telling fact about the Russian economy.

Continuing with my travels, I head two hours south of

Chelyabinsk on a winter Sunday through miles of birch forests. It is a dizzying trip, as the black-and-white bark flickers and flashes like a vibrating strobe light. I have a meeting with a "foreign agent." Yuri Gurman, a local activist, has been so named, with all the negative connotations involved, because he once represented a foreign-funded organization called Golos that monitors elections. His local branch no longer gets any foreign money, but he is still regularly cited in the local media as a spy and a traitor.

The main road down to Khomutinino is surprisingly well paved, but once I arrive, the paving turns to mud. The village, a former collective farm with yet more cement one-story houses and aboveground gas pipes, has little to recommend it at first glance, except for a new wooden Orthodox church built on the foundations of one torn down in 1937. An elderly woman, bundled up against the wind, stands outside, clearly looking for someone. We dance around each other. I had been expecting Yuri, but with a newborn and a young son to manage, he has sent his mother instead. After she and I finally make contact, she fetches a huge key from her pocket to unlock the church door, revealing a simple rustic interior with icons hanging on pine walls. Some are new; others had been salvaged from the former church before it was destroyed, and lovingly safeguarded in people's houses over the decades. In stark contrast to the formality and gilt of urban churches, it is intimate and inviting. A priest and his family used to live next door in a former school. A wreck of a place with peeling walls and encroaching damp, the school served as a temporary church and their residence while he oversaw the construction. He has since moved on to another community but comes here when he can to hold services.

Yuri's mother feeds some of the Orthodox cats, and we then head off to the family house, even more inviting on this chilly winter day. It's an ingenious concoction of Soviet cement, scrap metal, scavenged wood, and fantasy. Behind the inevitable walls that now surround most houses for security and privacy, there is a small courtyard with a barbecue pit, fruit trees, a fanciful plastic-lined fishpond, a traditional Russian sauna, and the remnants of last summer's garden. What is proudly and somewhat conspiratorially called "an American billiard table"—a story for another day—takes up the entrance hall, one of the few places where village youth can come for entertainment. The main room has beds along the walls, a bar well stocked with "home brew," and a large dining table groaning with dumplings, beet sauce, salted fish, and slabs of fat I am repeatedly told goes well with vodka. *Sala*, however, is the one Russian dish I have yet to appreciate.

Settling his young son with Legos, Yuri finally joins his family and local friends. He grew up here and is looking for ways to attract investment for this community of fifteen hundred to survive. He has formed an association of small towns that seek a greater say in their development. The perversity of the current situation is considerable. For example, the regional government recently decided Khomutinino needed to expand its school, even though it has fewer and fewer kids. Someone benefited from this, and it was not the community. Money appeared to restore the community center, but it was taken over by the local government for its offices. There is nowhere in the village to hold community events. I couldn't find a shop or a café.

Yuri got several mayors to sign a letter demanding a clearer, predictable budget process with input from local officials about how money will be used. It was immediately criticized by the regional government, and then most of the mayors promptly distanced themselves from the letter, fearing for their political lives.

When elections approached, members of Putin's party visited from the regional capital and threatened voters that if they did not vote for the Kremlin's party, all funding would be cut off. Yuri ran for office, and despite widespread vilification as an American spy he managed to get 36 percent of the vote.

The village was pillaged in the 1990s. The farm director

refused to divide up the collective's land as mandated and got away with it. It's since been privatized and locals work at a new badly run dairy farm for less than a hundred dollars a month. It's in debt. A sanatorium, where mostly state-subsidized patients recuperate after strokes and heart attacks, was also unscrupulously privatized and mismanaged and is also in debt. While it's hard to envisage the slovenly village as a tourist destination, Yuri hopes that villagers can turn their homes into B and Bs, offering local produce, home cooking, and a taste of village life. While the village has no charm, the surrounding birch and pine forests and three lakes, each with a different mineral composition, could be developed for medicinal and recreational uses. If anything good has come of the Ukrainian adventure, a campaign Yuri does not support, it could be a growth in domestic tourism. As ever, though, the region's reputation for pollution and the Soviet-style facilities are no help.

Yuri remains determined. But a close friend from Chelyabinsk, who moved out here to help him with his projects, is giving up. Irina Durmanova, a former journalist, says she's done everything possible to galvanize the locals to stand up for what is theirs and what they need, but after several years she has concluded they don't want to hear her message. "They remain utterly passive," she says. "I try to tell them that you are in fact the owners, but they don't get it. They are still slaves and don't understand what it means to be a citizen and have rights." Yuri, however, says it can't get worse than it is. He thinks it's so bad that people will wake up.

As one drives still farther south toward the border with Kazakhstan, the birch groves vanish, and the villages and towns grow ever more isolated. The vistas turn into breathtaking rolling steppe. This is the beginning of the vast expanses the Soviets called the Virgin Lands. In the 1950s and 1960s, the nation's young who were not working in the factories were dispatched here to settle and cultivate hundreds of thousands of acres. Most had no agricultural training. Roman the businessman's parents came out here to start from nothing. Living in dugouts and tents, they built villages, struggled to develop the land with inadequate resources, and watched as a failure to adopt anti-erosion measures led to millions of tons of soil simply blowing away. By the late 1990s, when subsidies ended and opportunities elsewhere beckoned, the young, like Roman, blew out of town, making their way while most of those left behind went nowhere.

One of the students I met at a Chelyabinsk university came from these borderlands. She too has no intention of ever returning. Ksiusha, with a long blond braid hanging over her shoulder, could be the poster child of Russia. She now teaches English, French, and Italian in one of the city's many language schools. She spent a semester in Italy. She wanted me to meet her father, someone she clearly admires. I wasn't sure what to expect, but given her determination that we meet, and her experience overseas, I thought he might be in the opposition.

We all met in a café. While his daughter has decamped to the city, Alexander Seleznyov still lives in Kizil, a five-hour drive south of Chelyabinsk, where he has developed a successful construction company. Having made some money and established a business, he hopes his children can take over (even though they don't want to stay in Kizil) because he wants to go back into public service.

Alexander has a solid square Russian face, with cold blue eyes. He is intrigued at meeting an American and keeps taking photographs, but he is clearly suspicious of me. He is quick to say he has nothing against the American people, but he believes the U.S. government is out to undermine his country. Once a good Communist, he came of age during the tempestuous 1980s and is now fifty-two. He had his children in the 1990s, when he had no idea how he would feed his family. He never wants to see his country so poor and so laid low again.

He supports Putin and his vision of a more muscular Russia.

He believes the sanctions against Russia will make his country better off. "Thank you," he says, "sanctions will make our agriculture stronger." He blames the West for Russia's drug problem, which is acute in his area along the porous border with central Asia. Like many other Russians, he believes the United States has deliberately encouraged poppy production during its tenure in Afghanistan to undermine his countrymen. He bristles at criticism of Joseph Stalin, insisting he was the man "for the moment." As for the purges, he says Stalin killed no one personally. "He renewed the country and made it stronger," he says. "Everything we have now is on the basis of what Stalin achieved," adding, "We are nothing without Putin."

Once a loyal Communist, and still a Stalin supporter, he has since been baptized. He has made sure his children are baptized. He has watched and supported his daughter as she specialized in foreign languages and studied in Europe. Today, they both support Putin's policies of confrontation and isolation.

■

From everything Alexander says, I get the impression that he wants to square an impossible circle. He admires Putin and his vertical power structure, and he is not concerned by limits on freedom of speech. Yet he understands he needs to empower his small part of Chelyabinsk so that it can think for itself, decide what it wants and needs, buck corruption, collect thousands of dollars in back taxes that were never collected due to incompetence, challenge Putin's loyalists in his region if need be, and stop the corrupt practice of pressuring businesses to pony up what the government won't. He readily admits that ordinary businesses, without "protection" and dependent on government contracts and contacts, are routinely forced to pay large sums to cover local social services that should be covered by tax revenues.

In essence, Alexander is talking about the rule of law. If it was to be better established, he says, local businesses would grow and hire more workers at decent wages. He wants to modernize agriculture in his area and knows what needs to be done to consolidate farms, create storage facilities, and improve marketing. On many pressing economic and social issues, he is in full agreement with many we have met in these pages . . . Roman, the businessman, the entrepreneurial farmers to the north in Ilinka, the beleaguered Dr. Reebin, even the dissident journalist Irina Gundareva and the "traitor" Yuri Gurman. But when it comes to defining democracy, or the threats to Russia and what its place in the world should be, he is no reformist. He is proud of Putin, and between him and those who dread their country's current course, there is an unbridgeable divide.